MUHAMMAD'S ALLAH

AHMED HULUSI

Copyright © 2012 **Ahmed Hulusi**
All rights reserved.
ISBN-10: 0615634885
ISBN-13: 978-0615634883

MUHAMMAD'S ALLAH

AHMED HULUSI

www.ahmedhulusi.org/en/

Translated by ALIYA ATALAY

ABOUT THE COVER

The black background of the front cover represents darkness and ignorance, while the white color of the letters represents light and knowledge.

The image is a Kufi calligraphy of the Word of Unity: *"La ilaha illallah; Muhammad Rasulullah"* which means,

"There is no concept such as 'god', there is only that which is denoted by the name Allah, and **Muhammad (SAW)** is the *Rasul* of this understanding."

The placement of the calligraphy, being on top and above everything else on the page, is a symbolic representation of the predominant importance this understanding holds in the author's life.

The green light, reflecting from the window of the Word of Unity, opens up from the darkness into luminosity to illustrate the light of Allah's *Rasul*. This light is embodied in the book's title through the author's pen and concretized as the color white, to depict the enlightenment the author aims to attain in this field. As the knowledge of Allah's *Rasul* disseminates, those who are able to evaluate this knowledge attain enlightenment, which is represented by the white background of the back cover.

TRANSLATOR'S PREFACE

Contrary to conventional perception and striking to established views, Muhammad (saw) declared "There is no *God*."

In fact, his primary message negated and nullified the concept of Godhood altogether.

Many might find this a contentious statement, and conceivably discomforting to their conditioned beliefs, but that does not change the truth that Muhammad (saw) *never proclaimed the existence of a God.*

To be precise, his words were: "There is no *God*. There is only **Allah**."

This statement, known in Islam as the Word of Unity, is commonly assumed to mean "there is/are no other God/s, there is only one God, and that God is Allah"... The simple truth is, nowhere in Muhammad's (saw) teachings is there any suggestion that Allah is a *God*.

In this book, Ahmed Hulusi presents a contrasting outlook to what has been *unquestionably* accepted for centuries as the Creed of Islam, urging us to question it:

If there is no *God*, then what is Allah?

If Allah is not a *God*, then to what did Muhammad (saw) refer by the name 'Allah'?

If the Allah we have so ardently and devotedly embraced is not the Allah that Muhammad (saw) was referring to, then who or what is *Muhammad's Allah...*?

Aliya Atalay
Raleigh, NC - USA
2012

CONTENTS

READ WITHOUT PREJUDICE

From a God who thinks like man, to man who thinks like Allah!

Based on centuries of conditioning, humanity has come to assume the existence of a God who thinks just like man. A God who can fall asleep or become absentminded while things can transpire without His awareness!

In response to such primitive thoughts, the Quran asserts that a **God** who sleeps or dozes does not exist... For thousands and thousands of years, humanity lived with the assumption of a God who thinks like man, who evaluates and judges like man... Though, from time to time, people of truth have received revelations and have come to remind mankind that such a God does not exist...

But how can one explain to a primitive minded person with limited understanding, who does not comprehend the fine truth in the expression **the servant of Allah** (*abd-Allah*) and instead thinks of him as God's subsidiary on earth, that the **servant of Allah is actually the being who most perfectly manifests the names and attributes of Allah!**

In heed of **Jesus'** (saw) words "**you think like a man, not like Allah**" the **servant of Allah** is **he who evaluates creation like Allah...** but how to explain this to those with limited comprehension...?

The venture of man is between these two points!

From a human-like God, to the servant of Allah!

Every individual exists to comprise a stage of this formation. Man forms the stage in which he will forever reside with his own activities and thoughts in this world.

If after reading this sentence one does not feel excitement or a shiver down his spine, leave him in his corporeality… let him continue his fleshly life with the satisfaction of his bodily pleasures! Let him listen to all of this as though it is some fairytale then turn back to his daily entertainments!

Where are we on the venture **between the human-like God to the servant of Allah?**

Peace and blessings to my friends who find this question important and valuable!

AHMED HULUSI

1

INTRODUCTION

This book is titled *Muhammad's Allah*!

Perhaps most of you will find it a little striking. You may wonder, 'why not just Allah? Why *Muhammad's* Allah?'

My purpose in writing this book is to explain, to the best of my knowledge and ability, that Allah is not a god (deity) and that this god-concept we have all come to embrace, as a result of misleading information and conditioning, is not the Allah expounded by Muhammad Mustapha (saw).

Everyone, from the most learned to the most ignorant, has a concept of God.

A God that we love, get angry with, judge and even accuse, at times, for doing wrong by us! We imagine this God, who sits on a star in the heavens or dwells somewhere in space, to be like a benevolent paternal figure or a majestic sultan!

Those with broader views (!) are well aware, of course, that such a God cannot exist and claim they do not believe in a God, proudly declaring themselves as atheists.

Whereas, neither the aforementioned believers who postulate a God with their hearsay knowledge and conditionings, nor the atheists who deny and reject the idea of a God, have any awareness of Allah as explained by Muhammad (saw)!

So what is the reality of **Allah** revealed by **Muhammad** (saw)?

I will try to explain to the best of my understanding, the One denoted by the name Allah, as disclosed to us by Muhammad (saw), in the way that he urged us to comprehend.

My starting point is the short **chapter of the Quran '*Al-Ikhlas*'.**

The chapter that begins with the verse "*Kul huwallahu ahad...*," **which every Muslim knows by memory, but only a few have a true understanding of its deeper meaning.**

The chapter that has been equated to one third of the value of the whole Quran!

An ignorant man is he who has no knowledge, a stupid man is he who knows not that he has no knowledge, and a fool is he who has no understanding of his lack of understanding. The Quran gives much importance to the **intellect** and always addresses the intelligent ones while condemning those who do not use their intellect. The Quran urges man to use their intellect in order to see and experience the truth.

Certain **literate** individuals, though lacking the ability to use their intellects to contemplate, nevertheless classify themselves as **intellectuals** and attempt to base their atheism on the **primitiveness** of the **Quranic God**, thereby revealing the actual level of their knowledge, or lack thereof.

Intelligent beings should feel compelled to research any topic in depth. Otherwise, their delusive denial based on incorrect information will only yield them unfavorable results.

Unfortunately, despite the fact that Muhammad (saw) approached the topic of religion by explicitly denouncing the concept of worshipping deities and openly claimed **Allah** as the only One, his message remains mostly misunderstood.

The West approach the One denoted by the name **Allah** as though Allah is a **greater God** than the ones they previously heard of, thereby veering far off course.

As for the Islamic world, sadly, they too remain unaware of the **Allah** revealed by Muhammad (saw), and have instead based their faiths on an exterior, heavenly God.

While many spend their time in endless debates about the forms and formalities of religion, the very essence of faith, that is, believing in Allah and the points mentioned in *Amantu*[1] are completely ignored. Consequently, the faith of the majority is founded on baseless falsehoods.

The foundation of Islam rests upon the phenomenon of **Allah**. **'There is no God to idolize and deify. There is only Allah!'** This expression clearly alludes to the fact that Allah is not a deity-God! Then, what is Allah?

This is the question Muhammad (saw) answered through the revelation of the Quran, as he tried to stop people from deifying and idolizing external gods, warning them against investing false hopes into fictional idols and endangering their future.

Muhammad (saw), who articulated the Quran to us, taught us there is no God, that there is only **Allah**; that there is a **System** present within life, by which those who fail to comply, are led to suffer the consequences of their own actions.

If we live with the awareness of the existence of afterlife, our primary concern should be to know Allah and the life awaiting us after death, so that we may prepare accordingly.

If, on the other hand, we spend our lives only for the purpose of accumulating worldly possessions and ignore investment for the life awaiting us after death, then let us know from now that we will never be able to compensate for our past.

Taking this into consideration, let us now try to understand the One denoted by the name **Allah** disclosed by Muhammad (saw). Let

---

[1] *'Amantu'* comprises the six fundamentals of Islamic belief. That is, to believe in:
1. Allah
2. The angels
3. The books
4. The prophets
5. Resurrection and life after death
6. Destiny/fate

us see who the **Allah** Muhammad (saw) wanted us to know really
is…

2

FROM GOD TO ALLAH

From a God who thinks like a man, to a man who thinks like Allah!

For centuries after centuries, mankind has found solace in the idea of **idolizing** and **deifying** an all-powerful being with whom refuge can be sought against the many calamities and events that leave mankind helpless and impotent.

This process of deification and seeking salvation and success from an outside source, has led mankind to turn towards numerous concepts of god/s with the hope of having their dreams and desires met. As such, various objects that were thought to be powerful enough to have the capacity to meet their demands were deemed as gods, and hence began the period of idolatry.

At first, the gods were identified from among certain stones, plants and animals on earth. However, once their mortal nature was recognized, and as Prophets and Rasuls came time and time again pointing to the absurdity of deifying these earthly objects, man gave up on earthly gods and turned his gaze towards the heavens. **This time, deifying certain heavenly objects or stars with specific influences as gods.**

Whenever man encountered an object or event that he could not solve or comprehend, it became a mysterious power for him, to which he eventually associated a concept of godhood. This concept of **an earthly or heavenly god** falls into direct contradiction with scientific knowledge and is nothing but postulation. The Quran rejects this assumption that goes against verified knowledge with its '*kalima-i tawhid*' (The Word of Unity), '**there is no god**'.

Man imprisoned himself in a cocoon when he idolized fire and heavenly bodies, all in supposition of a 'god'. In time and with conditionings from the environment, he began to lead a life completely devoid of contemplation. Enslavement was the price of this ignorance; he **became a slave to his gods** and this dependence became his reassurance.

Of course, this only led to the hardening of his cocoon, burrowing him further into darkness!

When Muhammad (saw) announced to be **Allah's Rasul** in Mecca, there were 360 different gods inside the **Kaaba** alone. That is, 360 idols! Mankind was finding solace in deifying 360 idols that represented 360 different gods, each with a different role.

They were not able to discern that such **earthly or heavenly gods could not exist**, simply because they had no idea of the vastness of the universe they were in!

They thought that **god sat on a star up in space** and watched over our world, sometimes interfering in our affairs, and sometimes quietly observing to examine us, all eventually to place those of his liking in heaven and cast the rest into hell.

Mankind has done a lot of nonsense in the name of pleasing earthly or heavenly gods. In fact, in Hadhrat Omar's words, they would make an idol to resemble their god with a cookie, then they would worship and deify this cookie-idol and then, with much appetite, they would sit and eat it! Even worse, they would bury their 8-year old daughters alive just to ingratiate themselves with their illusory gods!

God denotes the existence of a deity **beyond** the individual. A deity that bestows the wishes of individuals in exchange of being praised, glorified, and exalted!

A **God** that gives commands with which you must comply in order to earn his favor, so that he places you in his paradise and blesses you with plenty in the world. For if you oppose him by following your own free mind and free will, he will become your enemy and punish you by subjecting you to various sufferings!

While mankind was caught up in the deification of false and primitive gods, Muhammad (saw) received a revelation that announced him as **Allah's Rasul**, after which **he strived strenuously to stop people from deifying gods**. He told them:

THERE IS NO GOD. THERE IS ONLY ALLAH.

This reality has been termed as the *'kalima-i tawhid'* (the Word of Unity).

So what exactly does the **Word of Unity** mean?

3

THE MEANING OF THE WORD OF UNITY

The Word of Unity: *La ilaha illallah*, comprises the foundation of the **Islamic faith**.

Taken literally, it means: **There is no god, only Allah.**

If we evaluate its meaning... *La* means **No**, *ilaha* means **god**, i.e. **there is no god**.

Note that, the first part of the word of unity is a denunciation: **there is no god, there is no deity**, after which it establishes the reality *illa Allah*, **there is ONLY ALLAH!**

It is of paramount importance that we understand how big a mistake it would be to evaluate and translate this statement according to the colloquial language spoken by the Arab population today.

Let us give an example. The Arabic statement: *La rajulun **illa** Ali* can be translated literally as: 'There is no real man **except/but** Ali' or 'There is no man **like** Ali' or 'Among the men none are Ali's **alike**' (note that all of these statements denote there are in fact other men, but they are not *like* Ali). However, when the word *illa* is used in conjunction with the word **ALLAH** it does not mean 'a god *like* Allah', that is, it should not be understood as 'there other gods, but none are like Allah', as the very meaning denoted by the word **ALLAH** invalidates this supposition from the onset.

Just as the auxiliary verb **was** (*khaane*), when used in conjunction with **Allah**, loses its general meaning and is taken as the present simple tense, when the word **except** (*illa*) appears next to the word **Allah** it also loses its general connotation and is taken to mean **only**. Here is an example:

KhaanALLAhu gafurur rahiyma cannot be translated as '**Allah was Ghafur and Rahim**' as the qualities denoted by the Names of Allah cannot be subject to time; they are ever present and ever effective.

Similarly, *illa Allah* cannot mean **except Allah**, which denotes the existence of others, but must be understood as **only Allah**!

The compositional qualities of the One to which the word **Allah** refers, does not accept the existence of **another**, especially that *beside* itself.

Hence, *khaane*, *illa* and all other expressions that denote time and (other) existence must be construed appropriate to the meaning of Allah when used in conjunction with it. Otherwise, it will inevitably result in the conception of **a god beyond**!

Now examining the **Word of Unity: There is no God, there is only Allah** in light of this consideration, the first message that we are given is **There is no god**. Only after this definite denunciation we are told *ILLA ALLAH*. As explained above, because the word *illa* is used besides the word **Allah** the only correct construal of this statement can be **ONLY ALLAH** as opposed to **except Allah** or **but Allah** for there is no other being in existence to which Allah can be compared to or excluded from![2] Therefore, in order for the UNITY and ONENESS (non-duality) of the Islamic faith to be communicated correctly, the Word of Unity must be understood and translated accurately.

Indeed, there is only Allah, and Allah is not a god to be deified, idolized or worshipped, as per the message 'there is no god'! In fact, Allah isn't even a god that is beyond man and creation!

So, what is worship as opposed to servitude?

---

[2] More on this topic can be found in my book *What Did Muhammad Read?*

To deify or worship something necessitates the existence of a god. That is, the very act of worshipping someone or something means there is a **worshipper** and one that is **worshipped**. This leads to duality. There is a **you** as an individual, and then there is your god who is beyond you, and you worship this god. Clearly, this is an interaction between two parties. We may say then, that **worship**, in this context, refers to the collection of all the activities that are done in respect to this earthly or heavenly (exterior) God.

The phrase *ABDU HU* (HU's servant) in the *Kalima-i Shahadah* (the Word of Witness)[3], clearly indicates that servitude is necessarily to the Absolute Essence, that is, to HU.

As for the meaning of **servitude**... All output by an individual, based on his creation program and natural disposition, is termed **servitude**. As the 56th verse of chapter *Adh-Dhariyat* says:

> **"I have created the jinn and men only so that they may serve me** (by means of manifesting the qualities of my Names)."

As such, it is not possible for the creation of Allah to transgress the purpose of their existence. This verse indicates a clear verdict and its result. It is also pertinent to remember the verse:

> **"There is no animate creature but that He holds its forehead** (brain; the programming of the brain by the name *Al-Fatir*)." (Quran 11:56)

In point of fact, the verse **"it is You we serve"** in the opening chapter *al-Fatiha*, exposes the meaning 'we perform our duty by executing the necessary functions of our creational program and the purpose for which you have created us'.

> **"Say: 'Everyone acts according to his own creation program** (natural disposition).'" (Quran 17:84)

---

[3] The Word of Witness is the testifying of the Word of Unity. It literally means: *"I bear witness that there is no god, there is only Allah, and I bear witness that* Muhammad is HU's (Allah's) Rasul and Servant."

Servitude is the output of activity by individual manifestations, based on the creation program given to them by *Al-FATIR*. That is, when individuals live according to their natural disposition, they are **serving** the purpose of their creation.

Oblivious of **submission** or **rebellion**, all activities of all individuals can be thought of as **servitude**. Submission and rebellion are different types of servitude.

> **"The seven heavens** (all creation within the seven dimensions of consciousness) **and the earth** (the bodies) **and whatever is in them disclose (*tasbih*) Him** (manifest the structural qualities of His names by constantly changing states)**. And there is not a thing that does not disclose (*tasbih*) by His hamd, but you do not understand their** [way of, discourse, disposition] **disclosure."** (Quran 17:44)

Servitude in the form of *taat* is the pursuit of an individual trying to know his essence and origin.

Servitude in the form of rebelliousness, on the other hand, is the collection of activities that prevent and deprive the individual from the treasures within his essence, which leads to remorse.

Therefore, while servitude refers to a lifestyle befitting one's creational purpose, worship is the deification of a supposed god by honoring him and expecting him to grant your wishes in return.

Thus, it may be concluded that, **God is worshipped, while Allah is served.**

How then, should servitude to Allah be performed?

In order to answer this question one must first discern the *AHAD* quality of Allah. For if the *AHAD* quality is comprehended well, one can see (with foresight) that there is no duality in existence. The concept that **there is Allah, and there is *also* the universe (outside of Allah)** is obsolete.

In other words, the common approach that beyond and other than this cosmos there is a **God** is completely false.

Allah disclosed by Muhammad (saw) is not a god!

Allah disclosed by Muhammad (saw) is *AHAD* (ONE).

Allah disclosed by Muhammad (saw) is the possessor of infinite meanings, which He constantly observes!

The realm of observation is the realm of names.

In respect of His absolute essence he is *Wahid-ul Ahad* (The Absolute One).

In respect of His attributes, He is *Hayy* (The One who gives life to the Names and manifests them), *Aleem* (The One who, with the quality of His knowledge, infinitely knows everything in every dimension with all its facets.), *Mureed* (The Possessor of Absolute Will), *Qadir* (The absolutely boundless One who manifests and observes His knowledge without depending on causality), *Basir* (The One who is constantly observing His manifestations and evaluating their outputs), *Kalim* (The Discloser).

He possesses infinite meanings and qualities, which have all been expounded by Muhammad (saw).

This realm of activity referred to as the world of acts (*af'al*) can also be called the **perceived universe** as its existence depends on the sensory perception of man, angels and the jinn that reside within it. They constitute materialized manifestations of knowledge within Allah's knowledge.

To put it another way, everything in existence is essentially localized, densified apparitions of knowledge, which, according to the enlightened ones, haven't even sensed existence yet!

In short, nothing in the universe has an actual existence; their existence is only within the knowledge of Allah. To put it simply, they are **imaginary beings**!

No matter what age man lives in and what level of knowledge he has, based on his five senses, he can never perceive the actual essence (origin) of existence!

Knowledge based on the five senses will only take you to the infinite space and dimensions of the universes within the microcosm or the macrocosm. Knowledge based on the five senses will take you to the stars, the galaxies, the black holes and white holes and to other universes perhaps, but you will always pursue your life with the false belief of a god beyond...

In my book *Spirit, Man, Jinn* I had talked about the **alien beings** to which the older generations referred as **jinn**, and how they deceive and delude man, including depriving man from the reality of Allah by injecting false ideas and visions of **religion** and **reality**. I want to briefly touch upon this topic here also. Alien beings, or in Islamic terms, the jinn, are deficient in two areas of knowledge, and these are the areas from which they usually try to deprive their subjects. The first of these is the *AHAD* (oneness) quality of Allah and the second is fate, or destiny, which is the natural derivative of the Oneness of Allah.

The Unity (non-duality) aspect of the Islamic faith, that is, the system of belief explained by Muhammad (saw), is founded on the belief that there is no god to be deified and idolized (hence, there is no god-concept) and that people will inevitably face the consequences of their actions.

The Quran confirms this notion with various verses:

"And man will only accrue the results (consequences) **of his own labor (his own actions)."** (Quran 53:39)

"Indeed, you will be tasters of the painful punishment. And you will not be recompensed except for what you did (your own actions)." (Quran 37:38-39)

"And you will not be recompensed except for what you did (your own actions)." (Quran 36:54)

"And there are degrees for what they have done, so that they may be fully compensated for their deeds, without any injustice." (Quran 46:19)

Since, as the above verses point out, we will be recompensed for our deeds, we should urgently study and learn about the life awaiting us after death and understand what Allah really is. For the concept of Allah is what constitutes the foundation of religion.

Let us know that, without understanding the meaning of the name Allah, we can never correctly know the essence of existence. Indeed, man and the universe can only be addressed and understood after comprehending **Allah**. Otherwise, we will have to make do with local evaluations and be deprived of the essence of reality.

Let us now, with this awareness, explore the encrypted words that depict Allah in chapter *al-Ikhlas*...

4

UNDERSTANDING THE CHAPTER *AL-IKHLAS*

When **Muhammad** (saw) was asked: 'What is Allah?', Allah answered this question directly in the Quran, in the chapter *al-Ikhlas*:

> **"Say: 'Allah is** *Ahad* **(One). Allah is** *Samad* **(Absolute Self-Sufficient One in need of nothing and free from the concept of multiplicity, far from conceptualization and limitation).** **He begets not. Nor was He begotten. And there is none like unto Him.'"**

Let us first explore the general meaning of this chapter, which reveals the **Allah disclosed by Muhammad** (saw), and then have a deeper look at the implications it presents to us with its meanings.

Allah is *Ahad*... That is, Allah is **ONENESS** such that it cannot be broken down into parts or fragments.

Let us explore this notion a little further:

Every person on earth living under normal conditions evaluates existence via their five senses. Hence, the tool of measurement among human beings is the five-sense perception. Based on this, we assume to be living in a universe with a height, length and width. Consequently, no matter how much we may say **God is everywhere**, in actuality we still think of a **God** with spatial dimensions and locality.

However...

The Allah of which we have been notified is an illimitable, infinite existence that cannot be broken down into bits and parts; it is *bi kulli shay'in muheet*, i.e. **the very thing that encompasses thingness!**

I would like to take this opportunity to make an important note...

Though I had explained this in depth in my book *What Did Muhammad Read?*, I also want to briefly touch upon it here:

It is widely accepted that the most accurate and comprehensive interpretation of the Quran in Turkey is by the late Elmali Hamdi Yazir, which consists of nine volumes in total. In Volume 1, pages 42-43, the following information about the letter B can be found:

> *"Renowned interpreters claim that the letter B here denotes either 'specificity' or the preposition 'with' or else 'to seek help'... Based on this construal, the translation of the Basmalah (which begins with the letter B) should be: 'For, or on behalf of Allah, who is Rahman and Rahim' which implies contingency. This is an admission of 'vicegerency'. To begin an activity with the words 'ON behalf of Him' means 'I am engaging in this activity in relation to, as a vicegerent to, as the representative of, and as the agent of Him, therefore this activity is not mine or someone else's but only His.' This is the state of annihilation in Allah (fana fi-Allah) pertaining to the concept of Unity of Existence."*

Ahmed Avni Konuk, an important *Mawlawi* leader, also mentions the letter **B** in his construal of the *Bezels of Wisdom* by Ibn Arabi. The following is from page 191, volume 2, Marmara University Faculty of Theology Publications:

> *"The letter 'B' in 'Bi ibadihi' connotes 'contingency'. That is, Allah becomes manifest on the 'robe of existence' of his servants."*

If we have been able to grasp this secret regarding the letter **B** in the Quran, then let us contemplate a little...

Ahad, who cannot be broken down into parts or fragments, is either a limited **One**, in which case He must be sitting somewhere in space (!), or **He is an infinite, unlimited, whole One**, in which case, I repeat, there is nothing in existence other than Him!

To associate or assign another existence outside of, or alongside, that which is denoted by the name Allah, the *Ahad*, goes against not only the intellect and logic, but also reason and conscience!

Let us have a think...

If indeed, other than Allah, there is another existence, then where is the limit between Allah and this other existence? How and where can we draw the line?

Either, **existence is infinite, limitless and ONE**, other than which there is none!

Or, God has limits and parameters and is bound by location, residing somewhere in the universe...

The most crucial concept one must grasp here, is that of **limitlessness and endlessness**.

Let us now try and understand these terms not by length, height and width but rather, as a **state of existence**.

5

THINKING OUTSIDE THE BOX

According to us, or the **five-sensed** individuals, we live in a physical universe among countless other micro and macro universes within existence. This judgment, however, is formed as a result of the limited **data perceived by our senses**.

Whereas...

If our planet was placed under a microscope with a 60 billion fold magnification capacity and we were able to observe our planet under this lens, what will we see?

With a 1000x lens we can see not just every individual but the atomic structure of every individual unit on the planet... So imagine what happens when this magnification level reaches 60 billion! All objects that are perceived by our eyes, be it people, buildings or furniture, will completely disappear, and hence the visual interpretation of our brain will change completely.

Perhaps we will exclaim: 'Oh!? Nothing actually exists here! Look at this place; we can't see anything here except atoms and electrons, where has everything disappeared to?'

This would be the exclamation coming from the very brain that projected tangible people and furniture just before viewing things through the microscope! Indeed, the brain would be the same brain, but the plane and means of perception would have been dramatically increased in capacity.

Thus, the brain always interprets various data based on its existing means of perception first, thereby making judgments, for example, that people exist, but then, when its tools of perception increase, it changes this judgment to 'nothing exists here other than atoms and the electrons that are rotating around them'!

But, what if we were born into and had to live and die at this level of magnification? Would we still have believed in the existence of the physical things we believe exist today? Or, would we have believed the entire existence, including our world and the infinite space, to comprise a *single* unit of existence, composed of atoms?

If, for example, our brain received data, not from a 60 billion x lens but from an electron microscope with a 10 trillion x magnification lens, would we still have claimed the existence of individual units of objects and people? Or would we have perceived existence as a unitary, whole, indivisible ONE?

If I have been able to illustrate my point, then please allow me to stress the following:

In reality, existence is infinite, illimitable, unitary, indivisible, whole, **ONE**! This is *AHAD*! It has no partner or similitude, and nothing within the micro or macro realms of existence is outside of or other than it. It is **ALLAH, the** *AHAD*!

However, due to our present tools of perception, we seem to perceive this ONE as composed of multiple parts. This is because our brain draws its judgments based on extremely limited data received by the five senses. So if we, in effect, take these as mere *samples* – rather than absolute – from the infinite forms of existence in the universe, and try to contemplate on the vastness of existence based on these samples... If we can then embark on a dimensional journey into the depths of the structure of existence and encounter therein the universal essence... and then if we can observe the **dissolution** of our **selves** in that **Self**...

This is the first crucial point to be considered...

As for the second crucial point...

Since the Allah revealed by Muhammad (saw) is *AHAD*, **the infinite, limitless, indivisible ONE, and since this applies to every**

direction and dimension encompassed by all existence, at what point or place can a second form of existence be present? At which point can we draw a line to Allah the *Ahad*, and say up to here it Allah, after here it is I, or it or god?

Where can this external god that is other than the *AHAD ALLAH* be?

Inside or outside of **Allah**?!

6

NON-CENTRICITY

Allah is infinite and limitless...

Thus, it is impossible for **Allah** to have a *center*!

In order for something to have a center it must have defined parameters, so the intersection point of its corners can be called its center.

Whereas, **Allah** has no boundary!

If something has no boundaries it cannot have a center!

Hence, it follows that something without a center cannot have a core or shell, an interior or an exterior!

According to our five-sense perception and the **material** world we assume as a result of it, an object has inner and outer aspects: a core and a shell. But how can such concepts pertain to something that does not have a center?!

The **Quran** emphasizes this truth with the following verse:

> "**HU is the** *Al-Awwal* (The first and initial state of existence) **and** *Al-Akhir* (The infinitely subsequent One, to all manifestation), *Az-Zahir* (The self-evident One, the explicit, unequivocal and perceivable manifestation **and** *Al-Batin* (The unperceivable reality within the perceivable manifestation, the source of the unknown)." (Quran 57:3)

That is, concepts such as **the first**, **the subsequent**, **the outwardly explicit** and **the inwardly implicit** all pertain to the same reality; all of it is Allah. The manifest and the hidden are not different things; it is **our perception** that defines them as different. The **First**, the **Last**, the **Manifest** and the **Hidden** all point to ALLAH.

Whether you refer to Allah as the *Az-Zahir* or the *Al-Batin*, whether you call **Allah** *Al-Awwal* or the *Al-Akhir*, all of these terms denote the same reality.

But if we had six or seven or even twelve senses rather than five, our concept of explicit and implicit would have been entirely different! Perhaps we would have perceived what is external or manifest to us today as internal or hidden, or vice versa!

The limitless, infinite ONE denoted by the name Allah is free from concepts such as **explicit** and **implicit**. These concepts are only so *according* to our assumptions.

Indeed, how can the One who is beyond conceptualized limitations, such as explicit-implicit and beginning-end, possibly end somewhere at which point a second form of existence begins? Clearly this is not possible! Therefore, every point to which thoughts or imagination can reach contains only the Essence of Allah, the *Ahad*, with all of His compositional qualities and attributes!

He who believes in the existence of **another** can only do so as a result of a lack of deep contemplation! This in religious terms is called *shirq* or **duality**.

7

ALLAH IS FREE FROM REFLECTION

The topic of divine reflection (*tajalli*) is also very important...

Since Allah exists absolutely in every point and instance of existence, it follows that Allah does not have a reflection!

Reflection (*tajalli*) denotes manifestation, visualization or materialization. All of this, however, implies **duality**. We know that existence is ONE and everything transpires within this **ONE**. Hence, a **reflection** of this **ONE** cannot be conceivable.

The word **reflection** is employed only because of the inadequacy of language, as no word can duly contain the ONE.

In order for anything to have a reflection, it must first have a center, a core, an essence from which **meanings** can be reflected to the **place of reflection**, like the rays that permeate from the core of the sun. As such, Allah must also have a core in order to have a reflection. This is impossible! Allah is not a localized material entity to have a core. A reflection needs a central point from which it can originate, without this central point one cannot talk about a reflection.

Beyond this commonly accepted definition of the word **reflection**, its actual meaning pertinent to our topic is: **The projection of the Names as the world of acts during the**

observation of the qualities and meanings of the Names by Allah, in Allah's knowledge.

In the past certain masters employed the word **reflection** to denote this reality. My first book, published in 1967, is also named *Tecelliyat* which literally means **reflections** in the general sense. Such words are also used to aid those with the innate capability and aptitude to discover the essence of this truth.

Having made this clarification, let us now continue our exploration… Can **Allah** be worshipped? Who will worship **Allah**?

Muhammad (saw) said the following in regards to **Allah**:

"Allah WAS. And nothing other than Allah EXISTED."

Upon hearing this, the listeners relayed these words to Hadhrat **Ali**, to whom **Muhammad** (saw) referred as the **gate of knowledge** and awaited an explanation. Hadhrat Ali's response was:

"And it still is as it always was" (*"Al an kemaa kan"* in Arabic).

We can conclude from this that Allah is now what Allah was then, i.e. nothing about Allah has changed from then to now!

Taking a deeper look… The word *al* in Arabic means **the** in English. It denotes specificity rather than generalization. If one says **book** it means **a book**, as in any book. But when we say **the book** (*al kitab*) we are making a reference to a specific and known book. Hence, to say *al an* where *an* means **instant**, the reference is made to a specific and known instant. Hence we can restate the meaning of this phrase as:

The instant (that we are in now) is that instant! which means **The instant at which Allah WAS and nothing other than ALLAH existed is this very instant NOW!**

The concept of time is essentially only applicable to engendered existence. Only something that is created can have a beginning and end, a past, present and future… **Allah** is far beyond such concepts. Thus, it is inapplicable to think **Allah** was in such a state in the past but is in another state now! **Allah** is **forever** in the same state of perfection **at all times**.

In this sense, even if words such as **was** are employed in reference to Allah, it is up to us to construe this correctly as **beyond the concept of time, applicable to ALL times** or even **timeless**.

All of this alludes to the reality that the moment we are in now is the very moment that **Allah IS, and** *nothing other* **than Allah is!**

Nothing has come into existence *from* **Allah!**

The proof? The proof is within the chapter *al-Ikhlas*.

Since **Allah** is *Ahad*, a secondary form of existence cannot be possible! It is also impossible for Allah to be divided into parts across time.

Ahad is only valid for one single **instance**, denoted by the word *dahr*.

I am *dahr*!

Dahr **is the instance** that *Ahad* is itself.

Allah is *SAMAD*...

If we take an extensive look at the meaning of this word, we will see that *Samad* means the following:

A whole without any void or emptiness, impermeable, nothing penetrates into it, nothing extends out from it, pure and only![4]

As can be seen, all of the above are synonymous with and complement the meaning of *Ahad*.

The One with no void or defect, the impermeable One into which nothing can be inserted and from which nothing comes out, limitless, infinite, indivisible, not composed of parts or fragments, the ONE and ONLY *AHAD*.

Let us try to understand the Allah to which these words allude. Otherwise we can never stop worshipping the God we have created

---

[4] Abdullah Ibn Burayd narrates: *"As Samad allazi la jawfa lah"* in reference to this. The meaning of this can be found in the 9th volume of Elmali Hamdi Yazir's construal of the Quran, on pages 6306-6307.

in our minds and form part of **"those who did not appreciate Allah duly."** (Quran 6:91)

Additionally, *Samad* also means, the Absolute Self-Sufficient One beyond the concept of **need**.

Indeed, if nothing else other than Allah is in existence, how can Allah be in need of anything?

So then, whence came the *Ahad* Allah revealed by Muhammad (saw)?

How did this profound engendered existence and the numerous beings within originate from the *Ahad* **Allah** expounded by Muhammad (saw)?

Again, chapter *al-Ikhlas* has the answers:

LAM YALID WA LAM YULAD[5]...

8

ALLAH DOES NOT BEGET

What does this mean?

Could it be alluding to the act of **begetting**, as commonly known?

The word **beget** means to give birth to; to originate another form of existence that is like you from yourself. Anything that has the capacity to beget produces another being **like itself**, from itself and carrying the same qualities as itself.

But **Allah does not beget!**

That is, **Allah** has not created another being from Himself! Or, no other being has originated into existence from the existence of **Allah**, as **Allah** is the indivisible **ONE**, the *AHAD*.

1. Allah is limitless and infinite, therefore it is not possible for 'another' thing to come into existence within or outside of Allah.

2. Allah is *AHAD*, and hence indivisible, which nullifies the possibility of **another** to originate from Him.

Therefore, it is not possible for **another** form of existence to have originated from **Allah**, even if it is with **Allah's** qualities.

Allah is not begotten and does not beget!

9

ALLAH IS NOT BEGOTTEN

Lam yulad, i.e. **not begotten**…

To be begotten from something, means to have originated from another being with the structural qualities of this being. This is the general usage of this word.

So if **Allah is not begotten** it clearly means that **Allah did not originate from another being!**

How can **Allah** have originated by another being if Allah is *AHAD*?

Allah is the infinite, limitless, indivisible **ONE** and ONLY.

To be able to think of another being from which Allah can originate, Allah must first have defined dimensions and parameters, such that we can ascertain His limits in order to determine the location of this other being.

ALLAH is *AHAD*. He is limitless, infinite and indivisible. He does not **end** at which point another being can **begin**.

As such, it is not possible for Allah to have originated from another being.

This is what *lam yalud* means.

The following verse *"lam yakun lahu kufuwan ahad"* can be interpreted as:

There is none like unto Him, within the micro or the macrocosm, nothing is in the likeness of the *AHAD*.

This is confirmed by the following verse once again:

"Nothing in existence within the micro or the macro planes is equivalent to HU!" (Quran 42:11)

10

ALLAH AS DEFINED IN THE QURAN

Let us now try to understand the **Allah** revealed by **Muhammad** (saw) in **the chapter *al-Ikhlas***, and see if **Allah** correlates with the god-concept in our minds…

KUL HU ALLAHU AHAD: **Say: ALLAH is *AHAD*.** Allah is the infinite, limitless and indivisible ONENESS.

ALLAHU SAMAD: **Allah is *SAMAD*.** Allah is the Absolute Self-Sufficient One, beyond any need or defect. Nothing can enter Him and nothing, no other form of existence, can come out from Him. Allah cannot be conceptualized!

LEM YELID: **He begets not.** No other form of existence has ever originated from Him, thus, there is no other.

LAM YULAD: **Nor was he begotten.** There is no other god or form of existence from which He could have originated.

LAM YAKUN LAHU KUFUWAN AHAD: **There is none like unto Him.** Nothing in the micro or macro planes of existence is equivalent or in resemblance of Him. He is **AHAD**.

All teachings pertaining to religion begin with the question: **What is Allah?**

Some answer this question by explaining the **god** they have created in their heads, and some by referring to the **Allah** disclosed by **Muhammad** (saw).

Since we are trying to delineate this topic according to the Allah taught by Muhammad (saw) let's try and understand the teachings imparted to us by Muhammad (saw) in regards to who and what Allah really is. So that we can clearly see that Allah has nothing to do with the concept of god with which we have been indoctrinated for ages.

The *AHAD* ALLAH taught to us by Muhammad (saw) is:

HAYY

ALEEM

MUREED

QADIR

SAMI

BASIR

KALIM

Therefore, the One **denoted by** the name Allah, who is *Ahad*, is the possessor of the attributes above. That is:

The One denoted by the name Allah is *AHAD*...

The One denoted by the name Allah is *HAYY*; limitless, infinite, indivisible **LIFE!**

The One denoted by the name Allah is *ALEEM*; limitless, infinite, indivisible **KNOWLEDGE**.

The One denoted by the name Allah is *MUREED*; dimensional, limitless, infinite, indivisible **WILL**.

The One denoted by the name Allah is *QADIR*; limitless, infinite, indivisible **POWER**.

The One denoted by the name Allah is *SAMI*; limitless, infinite, indivisible **PERCEIVER**.

The One denoted by the name Allah is *BASIR*; limitless, infinite, indivisible, the only **EVALUATOR**.

The One denoted by the name Allah is *KALIM*; limitless, infinite, indivisible totality of **MEANINGS**.

It is imperative that we understand that all of these Names and their compositions, be it *Ahad* and *Hayy*; *Aleem* and *Mureed*; or *Hayy* and *Qadir*, all point to the same and only **ALLAH**.

That is, all of these expressions pertain to the same unique **BEING**. They are merely different compositional qualities and attributes of the same **ONE**.

Allah, as revealed by Muhammad (saw) is such a One that He is beyond concepts such as beginning and end; He is infinite, limitless and indivisible, He possesses infinite meanings, and illimitable will, He is infinite power, there is no other than Him, He has no inner or outer, no core or center. In short, Allah is *AHAD*, the **ONE**!

In attempt to prevent a common misunderstanding among those who may not be familiar with this topic, I'd like to make the following clarification. In various places in the Quran, the word *ilah* (god) is mentioned, such as **our god** or **your god**, immediately after which it is stated that this **god** is Allah. In this case, it is natural for one to think Allah is a god. However, these kinds of statements are for those who believe in the god concept. Just like the warning **Allah does not sleep** is an answer given to those who believe in a god that sleeps. In other words, it is telling them:

The god you believe in does not exist. It is only Allah that exists. Your god, our god, is one and only; it is Allah alone!

All of this is to help rid people from their god illusion and to recognize ALLAH.

Indeed, if one studies the Quran properly, one may see that such warning have always come addressing the **dualists** (*mushrikun*), who fragment the One Reality by worshipping **gods** they assume outside of **ALLAH**, in order to guide them back to the unity of **ALLAH**.

11

ALLAH IS NOT A GOD

Let's consult our conscience and have a think...

Is the god in whom we have either believed or not believed, but in any case of whom we have been conditioned to think in a particular way, the same as the **Allah** that **Muhammad** (saw) disclosed?

Can the word or concept **god** even be applied to the Allah disclosed by Muhammad (saw)?

"And they did not duly appraise Allah." (Quran 6:91)

The place of **god** in the sight of Allah is the same as that of a servant! For, **both are forms of meanings in Allah's knowledge**.

For this reason, everything in the sight of Allah is **non-existent**. The Eternal One (*Baqi*) is only *wajhullah* (face of Allah), i.e. **that which pertains to Allah**.

"Everything will perish, save the face of HU." (Quran 28:88)

Every thing in terms of its **thingness** is **inexistent. Only the aspect that pertains to HU exists!**

"Wa yabka wajhu Rabbika Dhul Jalali Wal iqram"

"Forever will abide the face of your *Rabb* (the reality of the Names comprising your essence)**, the *Dhul-Jalali Wal-Ikram*.**" (Quran 55:27)

Only the meanings of the Names pertaining to *Dhul-Jalali Wal-Ikram*[6] are eternal.

"Fa aynama tuwallu fasamma wajhullah"

"So wherever you turn, there is the face of Allah." (Quran 2:115)

Wherever you look, you are face to face with the manifestations of the Names of Allah.

The word **face** (*wajh* in Arabic) can be used to denote more than one meaning.

If one was to say 'You will see the *wajh* of **Muhammad**' clearly this is referring to **Muhammad's** (saw) face. But when *wajh* is used in the Quran, it denotes another meaning. Though I had explained this in detail in other books, I would like to make a quick note here also.

The verse: *"Everything will perish, save the face of HU"* **should not be taken as a day, in terms of earthly time**, will come when everything will be destroyed... In the absolute doomsday, yes, this will come to pass. However, right now, we are concerned more about what it means to us in our present moment.

To perish is an act that is applicable to all times, including this very moment. According to the enlightened ones, this is observed **constantly**, evident by the verse *"So wherever you turn, there is the face of Allah"*.

The **secret** here is: Due to the lack of insight, many are not able to observe the **face** of Allah, who comprises the essence of every form of existence.

---

[6] The One who makes individuals experience their 'nothingness' by enabling them to comprehend the reality that they were created from 'naught' and then bestowing them 'Eternity' by allowing them to observe the manifestations of the Names comprising their essence.

Indeed, wherever you turn with your insight and consciousness you can observe the face of the Divine, as He is **Eternal** and **Omnipresent**!

That is, Allah is eternally present yesterday, today, tomorrow and forever!

The biggest veil for the divine face is the **label** or **name** that is given to a particular thing. This label becomes a veil to the meaning of the **face**. The existence behind the veil and the meanings that constitute it obtains its existence from the meanings of **Allah's** Names.

12

WHAT IS SELF-CRUELTY?

Whoever we call upon with whatever Name, we will always be invoking the One denoted by **Allah**.

The One denoted by the name **Allah** is such that it is impossible to speak of another than He.

Whether it be by His essential attributes, the meanings that He manifests, or the activities that are formed by these meanings, in every moment and in every way it is always He that is being thought and spoken of. **Any instant in which we think of or talk about another form of existence we assume exists outside of Allah, we fall into duality**. This is what the Quran refers to as *shirq*!

"**Do not turn to a god** (exterior manifestations of power) **besides Allah**." (Quran 28:88)

"**...Indeed, association** (partners with Allah, i.e. duality) **is great injustice**." (Quran 31:13)

Why is *shirq* **cruelty** and to whom is it directed?

It is **cruelty** to our essential selves as, by worshipping other god(s) **beyond** our **selves** in a veiled state from our essence, we are associating partners to **Allah**, thereby committing *shirq*. This in turn is depriving us from reaching the infinite qualities residing in our very own essence. Hence, we are doing the biggest **cruelty** to ourselves.

To be deprived of the reality of our own **self** is the biggest cruelty that can be done to us. And by failing to comply with the system, we are unfortunately doing this to ourselves.

The rule '**He who knows himself not, knows not his *Rabb*'** is derived from the warning '**He who knows himself, knows the reality of the Names comprising his essence (*Rabb*)**. To know **Allah**, one must understand the **One denoted by the name Allah**. This understanding can only be acquired by the knowledge of **Allah** disclosed by **Muhammad** (saw).

I had intricately covered the topic of **self** in *Know Yourself*, but I shall also talk a little about it here.

Since there is no other existence but **Allah**, who or what is this existence to which we refer as the **self** or as **I**? How was it formed?

What clues have we been provided with to help us resolve this?

We will try to answer these questions in congruence with the understanding of Allah we have been sharing so far. If we say anything to contradict that which has been said up to this point, we will automatically be misled and fall into the trap of duality; **the person *and* his god**.

The Quran states the following regarding the creation purpose of human beings:

"**...And when your *Rabb* said to the angels, 'Indeed, I will make upon the earth** (the body) **a vicegerent** (conscious beings who will live with the awareness of the Names).'" (Quran 2:30)

It is interesting to note that man has been made a **vicegerent upon the earth** and not the universe or cosmos.

But how did man become a **vicegerent**? The Quran answers this with the verse:

"**And He taught Adam** (a manifested and programmed composition of the Names) **all of the Names** (all knowledge pertaining to the Names and their manifestation)..." (Quran 2:31)

What this verse is saying is:

Man has been endowed with the capacity and capability to manifest the infinite Names of Allah, to the extent that he wills. This endowment is what the verse above refers to as **He taught Adam,** i.e. **He endowed man with the innate capacity and capability to manifest the Names of Allah.**

But how did man, equipped with such capacity, and the universe in which he lives, come about in the first place?

If **Allah** does not reflect and nothing comes out of Allah, then how and from where did the engendered existence that our five senses perceives come about? And the angels, jinn, heaven and hell? The Intermediary Realm (*barzakh*) explained in the **Quran** and countless other forms of existence... How did they all come to exist?

13

HOW DOES MULTIPLICITY ARISE FROM UNITY?

Since the One denoted by the name Allah is the ONLY existence, how did the seeming multiplicities form? If existence is originally within the knowledge of the One, how did the engendered existence come about? How did these **imaginary** forms of existence, comprising the **assumed world** or **illusionary creation** come to be?

I want to simplify this by way of an example. It cannot be applied to the One denoted by the name Allah, of course, but it will give us some clarification.

Imagine a world in which there is a rich, a poor, a beautiful and an ugly... Equip these people in your imagination with various attributes and then leave them to interact with each other...

Do these imaginary beings that you have created in your mind have independent existence? Obviously not! From where do they obtain their existence? From you! You have created them in your mind! To whom do their attributes and qualities belong? To you! You formed them and their qualities!

So can I take a look at these imagined beings and define you according to them? Can I claim **you are the sum total of these qualities**? No! Just as you have assigned these qualities to these forms, you could be assigning completely different qualities to other forms...

Remember, they owe their existence to you, they are non-existent without you, hence all of their qualities and attributes belong to you. You are the one who formed their qualities! Just as they don't have independent existence without you, they don't have any attributes that are independent of you either!

Nevertheless, I cannot confine you to these qualities, I cannot claim you exist with or comprise these qualities alone!

Let us try to understand the engendered existence and all the multiplicities it comprises by way of this example...

The One denoted by the name Allah, the absolute possessor of infinite, limitless knowledge and power, has created the multiplicities with the infinite structural qualities he created in His consciousness!

We are individuals created in the knowledge of Allah!

Our whole existence and all of our qualities belong to Allah, however, **Allah cannot be defined with or confined by these qualities and attributes; Allah is beyond all comparison, definition and resemblance!**

If we can understand this, we will see that, essentially, **we are NOTHING in the sight of Allah**.

How much can a piece of artwork encapsulate its artist?

An artist may have a moment of inspiration and produce an incredible artwork. But this piece can only be the reflection of the artist's frame of mind at that time, perhaps the reflection of only a moment of inspiration! Surely, it cannot be a depiction of the artist as a whole!

The whole universe, with all of mankind, from the first human beings to now... all of creation, everything comprising the earth, our solar system, the 400 billion stars in our galaxy (in which our solar system is like a grain of sand)... and the entire cosmos composed of billions of galaxies, everything that we can perceive, **the infinite, vast space, all of it, is a depiction of only a thought of one INSTANT in the sight of Allah**.

Our UNIVERSE, or what we perceive as this infinite limitless existence comprising the whole of creation, to which Sufism refers with various titles like the Perfect Man (*Al-Insan Al-Kamil*), the Grand Spirit (*Ruh-ul Azam*) and the First Intellect (*Aql-i Awwal*), is nothing but **an INSTANTANEOUS CREATION in the sight of Allah**. Our cosmos, which we perceive to be infinite and everything in it, is the result of this creation of an instance!

Just as a human body is formed from one single cell, the whole cosmos is formed from one instance of a thought. Just as the whole of the creation program is contained in that one single original cell, the complete creational plan and program of the whole universe and everything in it is contained in that single instance of observation. This is the reality of destiny.

So if all of this is the projection of only a single instance, imagine the infinite universes contained within the **infinite instances** in Allah's knowledge.

Let's think about the letter **K**. Imagine the vertical line comprising this letter extended to infinity; that it had no beginning and no end. Now think of a single point on this line, from which the second and third lines extend to form the letter **K**. If we think of this infinitely long vertical line as Allah's knowledge, we may say the angle formed by the second and third lines, which originate from a single point (an instance) on this line, is like our universe. Note that I am saying **angle** and not a triangle, since a triangle has defined boundaries, as opposed to our universe, which is dimensionally infinite.

This infinite existence has been created in a single instance in Allah's knowledge. Creation has no limits and this limitless boundless reflection comprises only a single **instance**. And there are countless other universes within countless other instances as such! The vertical line of the letter K constitutes infinite points and everything we perceive, the entire universe, is nothing other than the observation of a single point on this line. Every single universe among the infinite universes is an artwork of Allah's creative knowledge.

As the angels perfectly state in the Quran:

"We can only know you with the knowledge you grant us."

That is, 'we can only know you, with the knowledge, consciousness and comprehension with which you have bestowed us; it is not possible for us to really know you!'

In the knowledge of Allah, we are but forms of imagination, among infinite others!

Everything that projects as these forms are all created by Allah.

"...While Allah created you and that which you do." (Quran 37:96)

It is not difficult to understand this. Think about the example I gave previously. Think about those forms you have created in your imagination and allow them to interact with each other. When they meet one another and display certain behaviors, will their separate independent existence drive their behavior? Or will they be displaying the natural activities of the attributes with which you have designed them? Obviously the latter! Hence, we, as the creation of Allah, are only agents manifesting Allah's qualities and will. And this very act of manifesting Allah's qualities is the reality of **servitude!**

How much can I know you or you know me? I can only know you as much as myself. And you can only know me as much as yourself. If I possess a quality that you lack, then you can never know that particular quality of mine. And if I lacked a quality that you had, I will never know you with that quality.

If within this universe there is another universe of which we lack perception, then we can never discern it. So if we think in this light... We can only know the infinite existence denoted by the name Allah as much as He reflects on us. In fact, Allah's infiniteness is only so according to the meanings projecting on us. **In reality, Allah is even beyond concepts such as infinite and limitless.**

Though I gave the letter K as an example to elucidate this topic, one should not understand it as only one line of infinite points. It should be thought of as a platform of infinity. For even an infinite

line has boundaries. Think of it, perhaps, as an infinite space full of infinite points and our universe as only one of these points.

Now, let's take it one notch further... Think of the angle forming from one of those points and try to grasp its infiniteness... Now in this dimensionally infinite angle, there are countless other points, and each of these points also project infinite angles... In other words, angles, within angles, within angles, all within a single point, in a space of infinite points! Such is creation!

14

THE 'POINT'

It is said:

What begins at the point ends at the alif⁷.

That is, everything begins at the point of **Oneness** (*ahadiyyah*) and ends at the *alif* of **Unity** (*wahidiyyah*). The whole of existence is only one reflection, referred in Sufism as the **One Theophany** or the Divine Self-disclosure of Allah (*Tajalli Wahid*).

It is also said:

What begins at the point ends at the sīn⁸.

Where *sīn* means **human** in Arabic and the point is the **One** (*Ahad*).

The Quran begins with the letter *bā⁹* of the *Basmalah¹⁰*. To be more precise, the point beneath the *bā*. When this point is extended it becomes an *alif*!

Just like when one wants to draw a line one begins at a point, which then becomes the source from which the line extends. The *bā* of the *Basmalah* is the source point of all of the characters in the

---

⁷ *Alif* (ا) is the first letter of the Arabic alphabet and represents unity depicted by its single stroke.
⁸ *Sīn* (س) is the twelfth letter of the Arabic alphabet. As a word 'sīn' means 'man' or 'human.'
⁹ '*Bā*' (ب) is the second letter of the Arabic alphabet, and the first letter of the Quran. It holds a symbolic value in Hadhrat Ali's acclaimed saying "I am the point beneath the *bā*", the point referring to individual experience being the result of their intrinsic reality.
¹⁰ The *Basmalah* is an Arabic noun used to refer to the Quranic phrase "*b-ismi-Allah-er-Rahman-er-Rahim*" found in the beginning of every chapter of the Quran, which literally means "In the name of Allah who is *Rahman* and *Rahim*."

Quran. The point never changes. Every character is a series of points that come together and seem like lines. In their essence, they are repetitions of the same point!

Hadhrat Ali says:

> "*I am the point beneath the bā*", perhaps to mean, "*I am none, yet I am all... I am the alif.*"

The last chapter of the Quran is called *Nâs*, which means **mankind**. As mentioned, the letter sīn is representative of a single human. Hence, the chapter *Yasīn* means **O humans** (or O mankind).

Eventually what we have is a semi-circle, going from the point to man, and the journey of man through consciousness back to the point.

Uniting with Allah, in essence, comes about in man with the knowledge of the point.

Will the knowledge of the point make mankind (*nâs*) obsolete?

Since, in terms of their actual reality, humans do not have an independent existence, it makes no sense to talk about losing something that doesn't exist in the first place.

The Earth...

And the sun, to which the Earth is bound, 1,333,000 times bigger than the Earth...

A galaxy comprised of 400 billion stars like the sun...

The Universe, which contains billions of such galaxies...

Infinite other universes that are perceived by infinite other systems of perception...

Universes within universes...

And finally, a single point, forming the angle, from which all of these infinite universes originate... A **single POINT**, a **single INSTANCE**... *DAHR*!

The name **ALLAH**... to denote the creator of these infinite points, instances, and all the angles projecting from them to form the infinite number of universes within universes!

15

NAMES

The word Allah is a name!

A name is a word that points and Allah is **not** a name that points to a god.

Indeed, this name is not used in reference to the concept of god at all!

This name is used to direct our attention somewhere; we are asked to contemplate on what the name Allah **points to**, so that we may decipher the truth…

Now, if you had read a few of my books, or had seen my photo somewhere, and somebody asked you 'Do you know Hulusi?', how realistic would your answer be if you say 'Yes, I know him'? How much can a photo and a few books, which depict some of my thoughts at some interval of my life, reveal about my personality? People spend a lifetime together and still don't know each other! All you can really know about Hulusi, based on these, is his physical looks and that he is a Sufi.

How much can an artwork depict its artist? All that can be captured in an artwork is the thoughts and imagination of the artist **at the time of making the artwork**. Nothing more.

And how about the personality of the artist? Unknown!

So if the name Hulusi is only a reference word pointing to the author of these books, and if it is not possible to know who Hulusi is based on his name, then similarly, it is also impossible to know the existence denoted by the name Allah, based on His name alone.

So if the word Allah is only a name that is used to channel our understanding to a particular reality, what is this reality of which we need to be aware?

If we remember that the word of unity, *La ilaha illallah*, **denounces all concepts of god** and claims it is only Allah that exists, then it follows that:

All perceivable and unperceivable things by mankind, that is, **all relative and absolute planes of existence**, are a projection of a single instance in the sight of **Allah**! It is only **one instance**, according to HU, among infinite others!

Everything that we perceive, not perceive, recognize, fail to recognize, design or imagine, are all contained within this single instance of projection of the One denoted by the name Allah.

This instance is a **point** in the sight of HU.

This point, according to us, is the source point of manifestation.

Humanity, the jinn, the angels, and all of the universes within universes of perception, have all been manifested from this single point.

Ponder on a single point amid infinity!

Created as the **point**, the universal existence is the **First Intellect** (*Aql-i Awwal*) in terms of its knowledge; it is the **Grand Spirit** (*Ruh-ul Azam*) in terms of its life, the **Reality of Muhammad** (*Haqiqat-i Muhammadiyyah*) by respect of its essence, and the **Perfect Man** (*Al-Insan Al-Kamil*) in terms of its personification. This is the existence denoted by the name **HU**!

However...

This personified existence is only a **form** of knowledge within the knowledge of Allah, who obtains his existence from the names of HU. Hence, his existence cannot be independent of the **point**.

All perceivable attributes and names, and the observable acts within the absolute universe that have been created from the point, are all due to **HU manifesting Himself every moment in yet another wondrous way**!

The **consciousness of the point** pertaining to the Perfect Man, who comprises only a single point or **instance** among infinite others in the sight of Allah, is beyond the knowledge of the one who has acquired the level of consciousness referred to as the **Pleasing Self** (*Nafs-i Mardhiya*) and is unlike the engendered existence.

The terms **infinite** and **limitless** only hold validity in respect of manifesting the names and attributes of HU through the Perfect Man; outside of the **point** they are obsolete.

Man, who obtained his existence within the point, has no existence at the point (*dahr*)!

Now, in light of all of this, let us reconsider the place of the word Allah, a reference word that points beyond the point to signify the infinite points in the sight of that which is BEYOND, in popular everyday language!..

16

THE POINT IS THE REALITY; THE PROJECTION IS THE ILLUSION!

All things that rotate most certainly rotate about a center. That is, at the center of everything that rotates lies an invisible **point**!

Everything within the micro and macro planes of existence is engaged in an active motion of rotation.

This is what the word *Subhanallah* signifies!

When one looks at a circle from outside one sees the circle and its center. In other words, **one** circle is observed as **two** things: the circumference and the center. Whereas, it is neither the circle nor the center that matters, but the **cone**!

In reality, the circle is a projection originating from the point. **The point is the actual; the projected circle is only an illusion.** That is, **the projection is formed from the point, with the knowledge of the point, inside the knowledge of the point.**

One who looks at the circle from outside will always see the circle and its center; one who looks from outside will always see **duality**.

One who loses his identity will observe the projection from the point with the one who observes from the point. He will be at the point of unity observing his own imagination. The concept of duality will lose all validity!

The idea of a circle and its center is actually an optical illusion. This is the illusion of those whose consciousness is enslaved by their organs!

The one who perceives as pure consciousness will observe the projection as **pure consciousness** as well. In the sight of the organ there is a line, in the sight of consciousness there are only points that comprise a line...

The point!

The projection...

Circles formed by lines comprised of points...

Points in rotation...

Points assumed to be in rotation...

Fa Subhan Allah!

17

THE REALITY DENOTED BY THE NAME HU

The Arabic word **HU** signifies dimensional independence, beyond all concepts of quantity and quality.

HU denotes the Oneness of Essence beneath the veil of multiplicity. The name HU references the *AHAD* quality at the **point**.

HU is the dimension of Oneness at the essence of the part.

It is this dimension of Oneness that forms the existence of individuals. It is the source of all existence!

The life contained in your fingertips is due to the blood and energy flowing from the veins of your arm. Thus, the movement and activity of your fingers is driven by the initiating signals from your arm.

Similarly, HU can be equated to **He** or the **Essence of the One**.

All that we can see through our physical eyes is included within the scope of the name *Az-Zahir* (The explicit, unequivocal and perceivable manifestation). The name *Al-Batin* (The unperceivable reality within the perceivable manifestation) on the other hand, references all those things that cannot be perceived via the eyes and ears or the other senses.

The totality of all this is the One, that is, all of this **seeming** multiplicity (which seems that way only because of the five sense perception) denote the One existence – HU!

Let's have a think…

Let's try to identify and recognize the essence of what we call **I**.

Let's turn to the essence of matter and zoom in to the levels of a molecule, an atom, a neutron, quark, quanta, and finally force ourselves to perceive things as waves of particles…

This zooming through dimensions is in fact the act of **Ascension** (*miraj*)!

The infinite cosmos in our perception is like an angle projected from a single point at a single instance. To restate, this infinitely vast existence we refer to as the cosmos or the universes within universes comprises only a single angle from a single point, of one instance among infinite others in the sight of HU!

The one referred to as the Perfect Man, or the Reality of Muhammad is also created from this single point. The point symbolizes the origin.

HU is the creator of infinite points and the point of abstraction within each point.

HU imagines into existence from the point, that is, from incorporeality.

Yet, HU is beyond and independant of all of this!

Such is the reality denoted by HU, intended for the realization of Muslims!

18

THE BRAIN

The brain is the mechanism with which we evaluate everything.

In terms of our current perception, the **brain** is a chemical composition.

This chemical composition carries out various functions via bioelectric activity to bring about all the formations in our existence.

In respect of the molecular structure of the brain, the biochemical make-up of its cells, especially those pertaining to the DNA and RNA molecules, allow the brain to be actively engaged in bioelectric activity, while simultaneously interacting with the cosmic rays comprising subatomic life forms.

To give a simple example, let us take the cosmic rays that radiate from the sun. These rays reach the earth from the sun in eight minutes and penetrate through every cell (and their sub-structures) in our body, causing multitudinous effects, all within milliseconds. These rays permeate through the whole Earth and continue their journey through space, every day, at all times. Throughout every second of our lives, we are constantly subjected to an uninterrupted flux of cosmic rays. Further, we are constantly prone to the radial cosmic influences coming from certain **constellations** (astrological signs) stimulating particular responses within the Earth and everything on it!

Unfortunately, humanity is still at a very primitive level in terms of deciphering this phenomenon.

Indeed, **our brain** receives these rays via the input receptors, such as the eyes, ears, nose, tongue, or perhaps even ones of which we are currently unaware, and interprets them based on its own evaluation.

The initial programming that occurs in the brain takes place in the womb. In fact, some even allude to the possibility of an earlier stage of coding, pertaining to the sperm and egg, before conception, based on the brain activity of the parents during intercourse. This, though, is on the periphery of our current topic. Those who are interested in further information about the early programming of the brain can resort to my book *The Mystery of Man*.

As we said, the brain is a data processing center. There is no vision or sound within the brain, just like there is no vision or sound inside the television unit. Like we consume food for energy, a TV consumes 220 volts of electricity for energy. The transistor, diodes, microchips and so on, comprise the center that processes incoming data. Waves containing radial data are received via the antenna or a cable broadcast, processed in this center, then reflected onto the screen and speakers as vision and sound.

Similarly, the brain receives its life energy as glucose and oxygen through the food we eat, and obtains its life force through the energy of the sun. Meanwhile, all the activities that take place in the brain are converted into waves and uploaded to our holographic wave body, known as the **spirit**.

The individual spirit begins to form in the womb, on the 120th day after conception. Hence, abortion after the 120th day is considered a grave sin in religion.

The Universal Spirit, of which the angels and the universe are comprised, is known as the Grand Spirit (*Ruh-ul Azam*) in Sufism. This Spirit, which was present before the universe came into existence, is a composition of Names, hence a totality of **meanings**, and the very first creation! It isn't a spirit in the absolute sense, of course... It is also known as the First Intellect (*Aql-i Awwal*) and the Reality of Muhammad (*Haqiqat-i Muhammadiyyah*).

No need to delve further regarding the spirit, as I already have done so in numerous other books. Unfortunately many find it difficult to digest the information I share about the spirit. Some people even question me 'How can you talk about the spirit, when even Muhammad (saw) was devoid of this knowledge?', ignorant of the fact that the Quranic verse **"little knowledge has been given to you regarding the topic of the spirit"** was not addressing the followers of Islam, but the Jews, who had asked this question in the first place!

In fact, Imam Ghazali, a renowned Islamic scholar and saint (*waliyy*), states the following about the spirit, in the section on prayer, in the 1st volume of his book *Ihya-u Ulumid'din*:

> *"Do not think Rasulullah (saw) was ignorant of the reality of the spirit. As, he who knows not his spirit, cannot know himself! And how can he, who is ignorant of himself, come to know his Rabb? Just as the Nabi and the Rasuls knew the reality of the spirit, it is not far from possibility that certain saints (waliyy) and scholars also had insight into this reality!"*

Going back to the topic of the brain, as stated above, the brain cells are constantly subjected to various cosmic rays while actively engaged in bioelectric activity, and thus its output of activity is based on all of these influences.

There are 120 billion neurons in the brain, each with 16,000 neural connections and each capable of carrying out all of the functions of every other cell! And humanity is only using 7-12% of this enormous capacity!

While we use this 7-12% not much is actually happening inside our brain! For example, when we see or hear, no sight or sound is taking place inside the brain. **The only thing that is really occurring in the brain is bioelectrical interaction among the neurons.**

Based on all the cosmic rays and environmental conditionings to which we are constantly subject, we have come to refer to the evaluation of certain data within the brain as **seeing**. But this is really just the value judgment of our brain! To say **I see** is no different to saying **I perceive**. For, in reality, it is the latter that is really happening; we are **perceiving** data and then interpreting it as vision.

As our tool and capacity of perception changes, so do the things we perceive, and the value judgments based on our perception!

In a sense, the brain is a mechanism that evaluates and interprets waves of various frequencies and cosmic rays in accordance with its internal programming.

While the brain uploads all this data to the holographic wave body it simultaneously produces, it also transmits this energy out to its surroundings, much like a radio transmitter. These transmitted waves of energy then become stored in the atmosphere, like a volume of waves, encoded by the transmitting brain. If a device can be invented to decode these stored data, the entire life of every single person can be screened and watched from beginning to end! As a matter of fact, religious texts that talk about the **books** containing all the stored information of people's lives and how they will be handed to people after Doomsday are not alluding to anything other than the decoding of these waves!

There are two ways to increase the perception ability of our brain. We can either invent new devices that can expand the brains capacity to perceive via the five senses or activate the brain's internal perception circuitry through various exercises, especially the one known as *dhikr*. The word *dhikr* (pronounced *zikir*) is commonly translated as "remembrance" and "invocation" or as "chanting" particular prayers and Names of Allah.[11]. Only after expanding and strengthening our field of perception can we begin to see what is currently invisible to us.

The pivotal point one should take note of here is: the brain is **unable** to evaluate and decipher the cosmic rays and waves of data it perceives if it has no existing information pertaining to them in the first place. Furthermore, if certain areas within the brain have not been activated, then all of the waves of data pertinent to these areas will be dismissed without being evaluated!

---

[11] More information is provided in chapter 24.

Our brain is constantly receiving streams of waves from the universe, all containing different meanings and information, but, due to our lack of decoding ability, most of these wavelengths containing valuable information are being discarded.

The whole cosmos with all its integral parts is a living, conscious existence!

Blessed are the ones who can perceive that the entire cosmos with all its multidimensional universes and waves and rays and quantal dimensions, is a unified, single unit of existence!

What we call **imagination** is this very structure with luminous origins. In fact, we are radial beings! Only because of the five-sense restriction do we fail to recognize this reality...

Indeed, by its origin, the universe is a SINGLE structure. And because all the particles are interconnected with each other within this structure, any one activity can bring about an infinite chain of reactions in any part of the universe! In other words, we are all connected; nothing in existence has a separate, independent, free will or existence!

This is where the phenomenon known as **fate** is derived.

So what exactly does Islam and Muhammad (saw) say about fate...?

19

THE MYSTERY OF FATE

There are countless verses and hadith confirming the predetermined nature of existence. Though I have covered this topic in detail in other books, I would like to mention some of these verses and hadith here:

"You cannot will unless Allah wills." (Quran 76:30)

"...While it is Allah who created you and all your doings." (Quran 37:96)

"We have created everything with its (written, programmed) ***qadar*** **(fate)."** (Quran 54:49)

"There is no living creature which He does not hold by its forehead (brain; the programming of the brain by the name *Al-Fatir*)." (Quran 11:56)

"Say: Everyone acts according to his creation program (*fitrah*)." (Quran 17:84)

"No calamity befalls you on earth (on your physical body and outer world) **or among yourselves** (your inner world) **that has not already been recorded in a book** (formed in the dimension of knowledge) **before We bring it into being! Indeed for Allah, this is easy.**

"We inform you of this in order that you don't despair over your losses or exult (in pride) **over what We have given you, for Allah does not like the boastful and the arrogant!"** (Quran 57:22-23)

The words of the Rasul of Allah (saw) regarding fate and predetermination are as follows:

Muslim (2653) narrated that 'Abdullah ibn 'Amr ibn al-'Aas said:

I heard the Rasul of Allah (saw) say:

"Allah wrote down the decrees of creation fifty thousand years before He created the heavens and the earth."

Muslim narrated that Tawus al-Yamani said: I found some of the companions of Rasulullah (saw), saying:

"Everything is by decree."

Tawus added: I heard Abdullah ibn Umar say that Rasulullah said:

"Everything is by decree – even incapacity and ability."

Narrated by Abu Huraira (r.a.):

Rasulullah (saw) said:

"Adam and Moses argued with each other. Moses said to Adam, 'You are Adam, whom Allah created with His own hands and blew into from His Spirit, yet your mistake expelled us from Paradise!' Adam said to him, 'You are Moses, whom Allah selected as a Rasul and to whom He spoke directly; yet you blame me for a thing which had already been written in my fate before my creation?'"

Rasulullah said twice:

"So, Adam evidently prevailed over Moses." (Sahih Bukhari Book: 55, Hadith: 621)

Abdullah (r.a.) said: "*Shaqi* (the unfortunate; the confined) is one who is a *shaqi* in his mother's womb, and the fortunate one is he who takes lessons from others' mistakes."

Upon hearing this, one of the listeners went to Huzaifa (r.a.) and explained it to him, asking: "How can someone be a sinner in his mother's womb when he hasn't even done anything?"

Huzaifa (r.a.) replied: "Why does this surprise you? I heard Rasulullah (saw) say:

"Forty two days after conception Allah appoints an angel to the womb. This angel shapes the child and gives it eyes, ears, skin, flesh, and bones.

Then the angel asks: 'O Allah! What should the gender of this child be?'

Allah ordains the gender, the angel records it.

Then the angel asks: 'O Allah, how long should this child's life span be?'

Allah ordains the life span, the angel records it.

Then the angel asks: 'O Allah! How about its sustenance?'

Again, Allah ordains as He wishes, the angel records it.

Then the angel comes forward with the page in his hand, having not added, nor subtracted anything from it, other than what Allah has ordained."

Anas (r.a.) narrates:

Rasulullah (saw) said:

"Allah appoints an angel to every womb, and the angel says, 'O Rabb! A drop of discharge (i.e. of semen), O Rabb! A clot, O Rabb! A piece of flesh.' And then, if Allah wishes to complete the child's creation, the angel will say. 'O Rabb! A male or a female? O Rabb! Wretched or blessed (in religion)? What will his livelihood be? What will his age be?' The angel writes all this while the child is in the womb of its mother." (Bukhari, Muslim)

Ali (r.a.) reported that one day Rasulullah (saw) was sitting with a twig in his hand and he was scratching the ground. Suddenly he raised his head and said:

"There is not one amongst you who has not been allotted his seat in Paradise or Hell."

They said: "O Rasul of Allah, then why struggle, why not let everything go and submit?" Thereupon he said:

"No, do perform good deeds, for everyone is facilitated in that for which he has been created."

Then he recited this verse:

"As for he who gives to the needy and seeks refuge in Allah and confirms the Word of Unity, We will facilitate him toward Paradise. But as for he who withholds and considers himself free of need and denies the Word of Unity, We will facilitate him toward Hell." (Bukhari, Muslim, Abu Dawud, Tirmidhi)

Jabir reported that Suriqa b. Malik b. Ju'shuin came and said: "Allah's Rasul, explain our religion to us (in a way) as if we have been created just now. Whatever deeds we do today, is it because of the fact they have been predetermined and written, or is it our doing that determines them?"

Thereupon he said:

"Everything has been predetermined and written."

(Suraqa b. Malik) said: "If it is so, then what is the use of doing good deeds?"

Rasulullah said:

"Act, for everyone is facilitated what he intends to do. He who does good will be facilitated towards the good." (Muslim, Tirmidhi)

Tirmidhi narrates:

Omar (r.a.) asked: "O Rasulullah, what do you say, are our activities created as we engage in them, or have they already been predestined?"

Rasulullah (saw) answered:

"O Hattab's son, everyone is facilitated to carry out that which has been predestined for him. He who is from the good will strive for the good, and he who is from the bad will strive for the bad!"

Imran b. Husain (r.a.) said:

Two people from the Muzaina tribe came to Rasulullah (saw) and asked:

"O Rasulullah! Were all the activities we partook in today predestined and written before we carried them out, or were they determined and recorded after we carried them out?"

Rasulullah (saw) said:

"No, everything has been predestined and preordained. The verse in the Book of the Exalted Allah confirms this: *'The self and the One who orders (fashions, guides) the self and shows the self how to do good and bad.'"* (Quran 91:7-8)

Abdulwahid b. Sulaim (r.a.) narrates:

"I came from Mecca and met with Ata b. Abi Rahah and asked him: "O Abu Muhammad, the people in Basra are saying there is no such thing as predetermining?"

Ata said: "Dear son, do you read the Quran?"

"Yes" I replied.

"Then recite chapter *Az-Zuhruf*" he said.

I began to recite: *"Ha-mim. By the clear Book, indeed we have made it an Arabic Quran so that you might understand. And indeed it is in the Mother of Books, in Our presence, high in dignity and full of wisdom."* (Quran 43:1-4)

Ata asked: "Do you know what the Mother of Books is?"

"Allah and His Rasul know better," I said.

Ata continued: "It is the book that Allah wrote before He created the heavens and the earth. In it, it writes about the Pharaoh and that he is of the people of hell, and in it there is the verse '*May the hands of Abu Lahab be ruined.*'"

Ata (r.a.) said: I met Al-Walid the son of 'Ubadah bin As-Samit the companion of Rasulullah (saw) and asked him: "What was your father's admonition when he died?" He said: "He called me and said: 'O my son! Be wary of Allah, and know that you can never heed Allah until you believe in Allah, and you believe in *Al-Qadar* – all of it – its good and its bad. If you die upon a belief other than this you will go to Hell.

Indeed I heard Rasulullah (saw) saying:

"Verily the FIRST of what Allah CREATED was the Pen. Then He said to it: 'Write.' It said: 'What should I write?' He said: 'Write *Al-Qadar*, what it is, and what shall be, until eternity.'" (Tirmidhi, Abu Dawud)

Abdullah b. Fairuz ad-Dailami says: "I came to Ubayy bin Ka'b and said: 'My mind is confused regarding the topic of fate. Tell me something by which Allah will remove the doubt and confusion from my heart' Ubayy replied: 'If Allah were to torment everything on the earth and in the heavens, He will not be cruel, and if He were to treat everything with His mercy (*Rahmah*) his Mercy would be more beneficial than their current activities. If you spend gold in the name of Allah as great as the Mount Uhud yet you do not believe in destiny, and you do not believe that whatever is decreed to afflict you will inevitably afflict you and whatever is decreed not to will never afflict you, Allah will not accept your benefaction. If you die upon a belief other than this, you will go to Hell.'

Abdullah Dailami says, 'then I went to Abdullah b. Ma'sud and he told the same thing. Then I went to Huzaifa b. Yaman and he told the same thing. Then I went to Zaid b. Sabit and he also narrated the same thing from Rasulullah (saw).'" (Abu Dawud)

Abdullah b. Amr (r.a.) narrates:

I heard Rasulullah (saw) say:

"Verily Allah created everything in darkness first, then he radiated His *Nur* (The Light of Knowledge that is the source and essence of everything) **upon them. Those who took their share of this *Nur* were rightly guided; those who were deprived of this *Nur* deviated from the right path. This is why I say the ink with which Allah's knowledge was written has dried, that is, everything has already been predetermined and destined, there is nothing more to write."** (Tirmidhi, Imam B. Hasan)

Abu Huraira narrates:

One day, as we were engaged in an argument about fate and destiny, Rasulullah (saw) came over. He got so angry that his cheeks went red as though pomegranate juice had spilled on them. He said:

"Is this what you have been ordered with? Is this what I have been sent to you for? When the people who came before you argued over the matters of fate they were destroyed. This, I swear to you, that you may not argue with each other, I swear to you!" (Tirmidhi)

Jabir (r.a.) narrates:

Rasulullah (saw) said:

"One is not considered to have faith if he does not believe in fate – with all its good and bad – and if he does not believe that what is destined to be, will be, and what is destined not to be, will never be." (Tirmidhi)

Aisha (r.a.) narrates:

Rasulullah (saw) said:

"There are six people I damn, who Allah and every past Rasul also damns. They are:

Those who add things to Allah's Book,

Those who do not confirm the reality of fate,

Those who exalt in rank the sinners who Allah degrades, and lowers in rank the pious ones who Allah honors,

Those who engage in forbidden acts in the harem of Mecca,

Those who do wrong by my family (*ahl al-bayt*[12]) and abandon my practices." (Sunnah)

Ummu Habiba (r.a.) said:

"O Allah! Extend my lifespan so that I may be beneficial to my husband Muhammad (saw), my father Abu Sufyan, and my brother Muawiya."

Whereupon Rasulullah said:

"You asked Allah for something in regards to predetermined lifespans, compulsory matters and predestined livelihood, all of which are fixed and not subject to change. Had you prayed for salvation from the torments of the grave and hellfire instead, it would have been more beneficial for you."

Upon this, a man asked:

"O Rasulullah! Are these monkeys and swine the monkeys and swine that have been transformed (from the human state, as a punishment)?"

Rasulullah (saw) answered:

"Verily, there is not one community of people whose lineage continues after Allah destroys them. These monkeys and swine are the monkeys and swine that existed in the past." (Muslim)

---

[12] Those who have been given the knowledge of reality.

Halid Al-Hazza (r.a.) said: "I asked Hasan Basri 'Was Adam created for the heavens or the earth?' Hasan Basri replied: 'For the earth'. I asked 'and what if he hadn't eaten from the forbidden tree?' he said 'that is not a possibility; he had to eat from that tree (as this was predestined)'. I said 'can you explain the meaning of the verse *"You cannot tempt [anyone] away from Him except he who is to enter the Hellfire."*' (Quran 37:162-163)

Hasan Basri said: "The devils cannot tempt anyone into delusion and wrongdoing other than those who are already destined by Allah to be of the people of Hell." (Abu Dawud)

Halid Al-Hazza (r.a.) narrates from Hasan Basri:

Halid Al-Hazza enquired about the verse *"for that He created them"* (Quran 11:119), Hasan basri replied: "He created them for Paradise and the others for Hell."

(Abu Dawud) Anas (r.a.) said: Rasulullah (saw) often made the prayer:

"O Allah, transformer of hearts, fix my heart stable upon the religion."

We asked him: "O Rasulullah! We believed in you and all your teachings, do you still fear for us?" He said:

"Yes, because the hearts are in between the two fingers of Allah, He changes and shapes them as he likes." (Tirmidhi)

Muslims says: "All the hearts of every human being is like one single heart, and it is in between the two fingers of Allah the *Rahman*; He changes it as He likes."

Abu Huraira (r.a.) narrates:

Rasulullah (saw) says:

"Every person is born into the religion of *fitrah* (natural disposition). Later on he becomes a Jew, a Christian or a polytheist based on the religion of his parents. Just like a

newborn animal that is so complete and perfect... do you ever see something missing?"

Abu Huraira (r.a.) said: "Read, if you like, the verse *'So direct your face toward the fitrah of Allah upon which He has created [all] people.'*" (Quran 30:30) (Bukhari, Muslim, Abu Dawud–Tirmidhi)

The tall man in Paradise is Abraham (saw). The children around him are the children who have died upon the religion of *fitrah*. One of the Muslims asked: "O Rasulullah (saw), are the children of the polytheists included among them?"

Rasulullah (saw) said:

"Yes, the children of the polytheists are included too." (Bukhari)

Abu Huraira (r.a.) narrates:

They asked Rasulullah (saw) about the state of the children of the polytheists (in the hereafter), whereupon he said:

"Allah knows best how they would have turned out had they not died as children." (Bukhari, Muslim, Tirmidhi)

Aisha (r.a.) narrates:

"A little child died and I said 'How happy for him, he is now a sparrow amongst the sparrows of Paradise.'"

Rasulullah (saw) said:

"Do you not know that Allah created both the Paradise and the Hell. Just as He created some for the former, He also created some for the latter!"

According to another narration, he said:

"Allah created some people for Paradise; He determined this while they were still in the spine of their father. Allah also created some people for Hell, and they too were determined for

this while still in the chime of their father." (Muslim – Abu Dawud)

Aisha (r.a.) narrates:

I asked Rasulullah (saw): "O Rasulullah! What is the state of the children of the believers (in the hereafter) who have died as children?"

"**They depend on their fathers**" he said.

"How can that be, when they have not lived to do anything?" I asked.

"**Allah knows the things they would have done had they lived**" he said.

"And what about the children of the unbelievers O Rasulullah?" I asked.

"**They too are dependent on their fathers**" he said.

"Without having done anything?" I asked.

He said: "**Allah knows best what they would have done had they lived**." (Abu Dawud)

Allah says:

"*And never would We punish a community before We send them a Rasul.*" (Quran 17:15)

Anas (r.a.) narrates:

A man asked: "O Rasulullah! Where is my father?"

Rasulullah (saw) said: "**Your father is in Hell.**"

After the man left, Rasulullah said: "**Your father and my father are both in fire.**" (Abu Dawud)

Zaid b. Sabit (r.a.) narrates:

Rasulullah (saw) was on a camel in the garden of the Najjar family when suddenly the camel got frightened and ran away, nearly causing Rasulullah (saw) to fall off. We then realized there were four or six graves in the garden. Rasulullah (saw) said: **"Does anybody know who are buried here?"**

"I know" said one of the men nearby.

"When did these people die?" asked Rasulullah.

"They died as polytheists in the state of duality" answered the man.

"The ummah (people) of Muhammad will be taken to account in their graves. If I knew you would not refrain from burying your deceased, I would pray to Allah to make you hear the sounds of torment coming from these graves as I am hearing them right now." (Muslim, Nesei)

Sahl (r.a.) narrates:

A reputable wealthy man, who helped the Muslims, joined Rasulullah (saw) in battle. Looking towards him, Rasulullah (saw) said:

"Whoever wants to see a man of hell should look at this man."

Upon this, one of us followed this wealthy man, who fought fiercely against the enemies of Islam. Eventually he was injured and to not endure the pain and die quickly he positioned his sword pointing towards his chest and leaned on the sword with all his body until the sword pierced through his chest and thus he committed suicide. The man who had followed him and saw this quickly ran back to Rasulullah (saw) and said: "I witness that you are truly the Rasul of Allah" (i.e. your verdict about this man was accurate).

"What happened?" asked Rasulullah (saw).

"You said whoever wants to see a man of hell should look at this man, while he was one of the biggest helpers of the Muslims. When you said this I understood that he was not going to die in this state. When he was injured he wanted to die quickly and so he killed himself."

Rasulullah said:

"Indeed one who is a person of Paradise (in the knowledge of Allah) will do the things of the people of hell, and one who is a person of hell will do the things of the people of paradise, yet what counts is the things they do at the end of their life (the state in which they die)." (Bukhari)

Abdullah b. Amr (r.a.) narrates:

Rasulullah (saw) came with two books in his hand and asked:

"Do you know what these books are?"

We said, "We do not know Rasulullah, but if you tell us we will learn."

Referring to the book in his right hand he said:

"This is a book written by the *Rabb* of the worlds (the source of the infinite meanings of the Names)**, it contains the names of the people of Paradise and the names of their fathers and forefathers (tribes)."**

And explained the attributes of these people to the end. Then he said:

"From now till eternity, no other name will be added to this list, nor will any name be taken out of it."

Upon this the apostles asked: "If this is a matter done and over then what is the point of doing anything?"

Rasulullah (saw) said:

"For, the people of Paradise will eventuate their lives by doing the things the people of Paradise do, while those of hell will end their lives doing the things the people of hell do."

Then he moved his hands as though he was throwing something and added:

"Allah has ordained and destined the fates of His servants. Some will go to heaven and some will go to hell."

Abu Huraira (r.a.) narrates:

Rasulullah (saw) said:

"In a time when people are believers in the morning and unbelievers by night, or unbelievers in the morning and believers by night, and when religion is sold in return of a small worldly gain, and when provocation (*fitna*) is like the waves of a dark night, run to good deeds!" (Muslim, Tirmidhi)

Abu Huraira (r.a.) narrates:

Rasulullah (saw) said:

"Prefer good deeds over seven things, for either one of these are awaiting you: poverty that strikes suddenly, wealth that leads to outrageousness, an ailment that afflicts your health, old age that makes you talk absurdly, death that comes suddenly, the *Dajjal* (Antichrist), or Doomsday, which is the most intense and difficult one of them all." (Tirmidhi)

Abu Huraira (r.a.) narrates:

Rasulullah (saw) said:

"Run to good deeds from six things: the sun rising from the West, the *Smoke, Antichrist (Dajjal)*, the Beast (*Dabbat'ul'Ardh*), from a provocation that comes (at death) or that prevents you from attending to others, or the Doomsday." (Muslim, Imam Ahmad)

Allah says:

"Fear me, if you are of those who believe in Allah." (Quran 3:175)

Abu Huraira (r.a.) narrates:

Rasulullah (saw) said:

"Hell is veiled by desire and heaven by hardship to the self." (Bukhari, Muslim, Tirmidhi)

Abdullah (r.a.) narrates:

Rasulullah (saw) said:

"**Heaven is closer to you than you think, and it is the same for hell.**" (Bukhari, Imam Ahmad)

Abu Huraira (r.a.) narrates:

Rasulullah (saw) said:

"**At the end of days, there will be men, who will prefer the world at the expense of their afterlife. They will cover themselves in sheepskin to seem mild, their speech will be sweeter than sugar, but their hearts will be as stiff as the hearts of wolves. In reference to them, Allah says: 'Do they think I am unaware? Are they scorning me? I swear by my might that I will send amongst them such a distraction that it will confuse them completely!'**" (Tirmidhi)

Abu Huraira (r.a.) narrates:

Rasulullah (saw) said:

"**There is not one person who dies and does not feel regret. If he had done good deeds, he regrets not doing more, if he were a sinner, he regrets not repenting.**" (Tirmidhi)

Abu Huraira (r.a.) narrates:

Rasulullah saw said:

"**He who fears (his enemy) will travel through the night and reach his destination, finding comfort and safety. Be wary! Allah's asset is heaven.**" (Tirmidhi)

Abu Huraira (r.a.) narrates:

Rasulullah (saw) said:

"He who cries in fear of Allah will not enter hell until the milk goes back into the nipple from which it came out (i.e. never). The dust that has been scattered in the way of Allah will never meet with the fire of hell." (Tirmidhi)

Hani (r.a.) narrates:

When Uthman (r.a.) stood near a grave he would cry until his beard was soaked. Someone once said to him "You do not weep when you hear about heaven and hell but you cry in front of this grave". He replied: "Rasulullah (saw) said:

'The grave is the first station of the afterlife, if one is able to pass this station the rest of his journey will be easier, but if one cannot pass this station, the rest of his journey will be more difficult.'

I have never encountered a scene more frightening than the grave." (Tirmidhi)

Abu Zarr (r.a.) narrates:

Rasulullah (saw) said:

"I see what you see not and hear what you hear not. The sky groaned and very rightly so, for there is not a four-finger space in which an angel is not prostrating upon its forehead. I swear by Allah, if you had known what I know you would have laughed less and cried more, you would have left seeking pleasure from your wives in bed and dashed outside in search of Allah's savior. (Rather than witnessing this) I would have liked to be a tree (cut-down and no longer existent) instead!" (Tirmidhi)

Allah says:

"He who places his trust in Allah, Allah will be sufficient for him." (Quran 65:3)

Ibn Abbas (r.a.) narrates:

Rasulullah (saw) said:

"**Seventy thousand people from my people (*ummah*) will go to Paradise unquestioned. These are: those who don't seek prayer for their sick, those who do not believe in bad-luck, and those who place their trust in Allah.**" (Bukhari, Muslim, Tirmidhi)

Omar (r.a.) narrates:

Rasulullah (saw) said:

"**Had you fully placed your trust in Allah you would have found your sustenance easily, like the birds who fly out hungry in the morning and fly back to their nests full by night.**" (Tirmidhi, Imam Ahmad, Hakim)

Anas (r.a.) narrates:

A man asked Rasulullah (saw): "O Rasulullah, shall I tie my camel first then trust in Allah, or shall I just trust in Allah without tying my camel?"

Rasulullah (saw) answered: "**Tie your camel first, then trust in Allah.**" (Tirmidhi)

Abdullah (r.a.) narrates:

Rasulullah (saw) said:

"**He who is poverty stricken and seeks the help of people shall never find the help he seeks. He who is poverty stricken and seeks the help of Allah, Allah will attend to his need sooner or later, or allow him a quick death to save him from poverty.**" (Tirmidhi)

Anas (r.a.) narrates:

"There were two brothers, one of them didn't work. Instead, he attended the meetings of Rasulullah (saw), while the other worked for a livelihood. When the brother who worked complained about the brother that didn't work, Rasulullah (saw) told him: '**Perhaps you are earning for the sake of your brother**.'" (Tirmidhi)

Muawiya wrote to Aisha (r.a.): "Please send me a letter with some short advice."

Aisha (r.a.) wrote to him:

"Peace be to you! I had heard Rasulullah (saw) say:

'**He who seeks the pleasure of Allah oblivious of people's anger (i.e. he who seeks to work in a way that pleases Allah), Allah will protect him from the wrath of people. And he who seeks the pleasure of people despite it causing displeasure to Allah, Allah will abandon him to the people (thereby he will incur a loss in every field).**'" (Tirmidhi)

"**Strive for that which is beneficial to you, seek help from Allah, do not be weak and incapable.**"

"**If something afflicts you, do not say 'if only I had done this, it would have been different' but rather, say 'it is the ordainment of Allah, and Allah does as He wishes.**'" (Majmu'atu'r-Rasaili'l Qubra)

Rasulullah (saw) said:

"**There is not one soul whose place in heaven or hell (whether he is of the fortunate or the unfortunate ones) is not already recorded by Allah,**"

Whereupon a man asked "O Rasulullah, should we then trust in our fate and not do any deeds?"

Rasulullah (saw) answered:

"**He who is of the fortunate ones will be drawn to the deeds of the fortunate ones, while he who is of the unfortunate ones will be drawn to the deeds of the unfortunate ones.**" (Bukhari, Muslim, Abu Dawud, Ibn Hanbali)

"**Act, for everyone is facilitated towards that for which he is destined.**" (Bukhari)

"**It is HU who shapes** (forms, programs) **you in the womb** (mother's womb – *Rahimiyyah* – the Names which comprise your essence) **as He wishes.**" (Quran 3:6)

"**Allah created everything in darkness then shone His Light** (*Nur*) **upon them. He who took a share of this Light became rightly guided and he who were deprived of this Light became misguided.**" (Hakaik, Timidhi)

"**And never will Allah fail to fulfill His promise.**" (Quran 3:9)

"**Allah will not make a change to what he ordained in His pre-eternal knowledge in regards to the fortunate and unfortunate ones, not due to the actions of the recluse, nor the reckless.**" (Hakaik)

Joseph:

"*No reproach shall be uttered today against you, Allah will forgive you... for He is the most merciful of the merciful.*" (Quran 12:92)

In regards to this verse, Abu Osman says: "A sinner should not be criticized for his sin."

Joseph said to his brothers:

"How can I criticize you? Me going to prison was preordained in Allah's pre-eternal knowledge. Indeed I made the mistake of asking my inmate to mention me to his master (when he was freed from prison). So how can I forget my own sin and criticize you instead?" Thus he makes it clear that these things pertain to fate. (Hakaik)

Shah Ibn Shur says:

"He who observes people through the eyes of the Reality (*Haq*) he will be saved from their opposition. He who observes people through his own eyes, he will spend his days in conflict and rivalry with people. Do you not see when Joseph realized he was afflicted with predestined misfortune; he accepted the apology of his brothers and told them "No reproach shall be uttered today against you." (Hakaik)

> "**Had your *Rabb*** (the reality of the Names comprising your essence) **willed, all those who live on earth would surely have attained faith, all of them...**" (Quran 10:99)

> "**And it is not for a soul to believe except by permission of Allah** (the Name composition which comprises his essence)." (Quran 10:100)

> "**Allah eliminates what He wills or confirms** (what He wills), **and with Him is the Mother of the Book** (primary KNOWLEDGE, the knowledge of the ways in which the Names will manifest at every instant)." (Quran 13:39)

> "**The judgment will not be altered by Me!**" (Quran 50:29)

> "**Whoever Allah guides, he is the one who reaches the reality.**" (Quran 7:178)

> "**Allah does as He wills!**" (Quran 14:27)

> "**He who Allah guides can never be led astray.**" (Quran 39:37)

Kasani says:

"The deeds of creation in comparison to the deeds of the Reality (*Haq*) are like the body to the spirit.

If the root of a deed is the spirit, the place of its manifestation is the body. As such, the creator of the deed is the Reality (*Haq*), though it becomes manifest through man." (Ta'wilat by Ibn Arabi)

Abdullah Ibn Masud (r.a.) narrates:

Rasulullah (saw) to whom the truth is revealed and who always speaks the truth, told me:

"Substance from your parents are gathered in the mother's womb for forty days, then in another forty day period it becomes a clot of blood, then in another forty day period it becomes a small flesh. (After the 120th day) **Allah sends an angel and asks it to record four things: Its livelihood, its sustenance, its death, and whether he will be of the fortunate or the unfortunate ones."**

Ibn Masud continues, "I swear to Allah in whose hands of power the life of Abdullah lies, after the angel records these, **the spirit is blown into it** (the fetus comes to life)".

One may do so many good deeds such that between him and Paradise will remain only an arm length yet at this point the record (written by the angel in the mother's womb) **will come and obstruct the person. After this, he will begin to do the deeds of the people of hell** (and be cast to hell).

One may do such bad deeds that between him and hell will remain only one step distance, yet at this point the record (written by the angel) **will come and obstruct the person. Then he will begin to do the deeds of the people of heaven** (and go to Paradise)." (Bukhari, Tajrid 1324)

Imran bin Husain (r.a.) narrates:

"Once I asked Rasulullah (saw): "O Rasulullah, can the people of paradise be distinguished from the people of hell (with the knowledge of Allah's preordainment)?"

Upon which Rasulullah (saw) said; **"Yes, they can be distinguished."**

"If the people of heaven and hell have already been predetermined then why should those who do good deeds and engage in prayers continue to do so?"

"Everyone will do what he has been created for, whatever has been predestined for him, he will carry that out" he answered. (Bukhari, Tajrid 2062)

Abu Huraira (r.a.) narrates:

Rasulullah (saw) said:

"An 'offering' will not bring the sons of Adam anything which they do not already expect, in fact, it is Allah's ordainment that attracts the sons of Adam. I weigh what ought to be given. With that judgment I will seek its attainments from the miser." (Bukhari- Tajrid 2066)

"O believers, when you are invited to that which enlivens you (the knowledge of the reality) **attend to Allah and Rasulullah's invitation. Know well, that** (if you do not attend to their invitation) **Allah will split the consciousness and the heart** (through the system of the brain) **and prevent him. You will be resurrected to Him."** (Quran 8:24)

As can be seen from Rasulullah's teachings, everything from the moment the universe came into being, till eternity, is known and determined. And nobody can change his destiny!

Everyone has to live his own fate. Indeed, the *AHAD* (inseparable) quality of Allah necessitates this to be so!

The Oneness of Allah and the failure to understand the fact that nothing other than Allah exists, has caused much debate about fate, leading to many inadequate ideas.

On the other hand, the reality of fate has been very clearly outlined by the verses and the hadith explained by Muhammad (saw).

Among the many scholars who assert that everything that happens to man is – without exception – the manifesting of one's fate is Imam Ghazali. In the second section of the second volume of his book *Ihya-u Ulumuddin*, he says:

> *"Because we say: 'all misfortune, rebellion, adultery, and even denial happen with Allah's **judgment**, will and wish; and rightfully so!'"*

20

ILLUSION

Let us now have a look at some of the reasons why the universe has been defined as an **illusion** or a **dream**...

The single unified existence, which we call the **universe**, is constantly and systematically manifesting its infinite intrinsic qualities in new ways. Hence, in relation to this primary luminous structure of the universe, our assumption of being material and our seemingly material world has been called an **illusion**. Indeed, Rasulullah (saw) asserted that this apparently physical world is only an **assumption** and that the actual structure of the universe is ethereal. Stressing that this material state of existence is only a **dream**, he said: '**People are asleep, with death they will awake!**'

One way of understanding this is: when man, living in a physical body, and limited by the five senses, makes the transition to the state of existence beyond matter, he will feel as though he has woken up from a dream, hence the world and all that he has lived in the world will be like a dream. In contrast, the radial state of existence he enters will become the real world. This will go on until Doomsday. After Doomsday, he will be resurrected for the third time into a new body, which he will use throughout the period after doomsday (*mahshar*).

The second way of understanding this statement is: based on the hadith **"die before you die"**, man must prepare himself for an immaterial state of existence by abandoning the belief that he is a

physical being and adopting the idea that he is an **intelligible** being. For, after the physical body and brain becomes inoperable, the spirit will no longer be able to acquire the things it has the chance to acquire during worldly life.

Yet another way of construing this hadith is: Die in terms of your illusory self, that is, by recognizing the imaginary and fictional nature of your seeming **self**, so that you may be enlivened by uniting with the Absolute Self who comprises your essence. For, 'I'-ness is exclusive to Allah alone!

Allah is the only One who can truly claim **I am**, as there is no other existence but He. If there were, then Allah would have been a **god**, whereas the Quran asserts: "**There is no god. There is only Allah.**"

Thus, Allah, the One and Only, in a manner of speaking, contemplated the corporeal worlds, or in other words, **imagined** them.

I repeat, using words such as **contemplate** and **imagined** in reference to Allah is inappropriate and inadequate in reflecting the reality of Allah; however, in order to expound and aid the understanding of the topic I have no other choice but to use them.

The universe and everything in it has been created in compliance with the unified assertion of all the enlightened beings who have attained and experienced the highest degrees of reality, and claimed 'the essence of the world is an illusion.'

Abdulkarim al Jili, an invaluable scholar with incredibly extensive knowledge pertaining to Allah and the dimensions and beings of the universe, quite comprehensively affirms the truth about the imaginary nature of the worlds in his book *The Perfect Man*.

So what is an **illusion**?

What does this word **illusion** exactly mean?

How is it formed? And why do we perceive illusions as reality?

The Ever-living One (*Hayy*) is, in simple terms, **aware** (or conscious) of His infinite qualities with the knowledge attribute denoted by His name *al-Aleem*.

Allah knows the infinite and limitless qualities He possesses. *Al-Aleem*, who **knows** His infinite qualities, **wills** to manifest and observe these qualities with the qualities of His name *al-Mureed*, and creates them with the **power** denoted by His name *al-Qadir*, and observes them through countless forms of **words** (manifestations) with His name *al-Kalim*.

Power is the ability to observe the inherent, implicit meanings! To encompass with knowledge all of one's intrinsic qualities!

If the seven oceans and the like were ink, it would still not suffice to write the words of **Allah**! How could it? It is infinite! What are the seven oceans, seven galaxies, 77 universes in comparison to **infinity**!?

Anything that can be represented by figures, no matter how large it may be, is nothing compared to infinity.

Allah is *as-Sami*. He is aware of every single **word** (meaning) He observes in and of Himself. Is it at all possible for Him not to be aware, when He is observing the meanings pertaining to His very Self?

Allah is *al-Basir*. He is the Perceiver and the Evaluator! How can He not be? It is HU, Himself who is perceiving and who is being perceived!

But where is this taking place?

In Allah's knowledge!

Though words are impotent from adequately expressing the reality, we have no choice but to employ them, and though insufficient, it can be stated that: 'everything that transpires takes place in the knowledge and imagination of the One denoted by the name Allah.'

Now we come to the second pivotal point:

If the above is true, then who am **I**? Who is 'me'? What is the **world**, what is the **afterlife**? What are heaven and hell? What do concepts such as **judgment**, **book**, and **torment of the grave** (*qabir*) mean? Who is making the proposal? To whom is it being proposed? What is the proposal?

Muhyiddin Ibn al-Arabi says:

> *"The servant is the Reality, the Rabb is the Reality!*
>
> *If only I knew who it is that is liable?*
>
> *If I say the servant, he is dead!*
>
> *If I say the Rabb, how can the Rabb be liable?"*

Pertaining to the same topic, **Imam Ghazali**, an invaluable Islamic scholar and saint (*waliyy*) who lived much earlier than **Ibn al-Arabi**, says:

> *"The enlightened ones will elevate from the pit of metaphor to the pinnacle of reality, completing their ascension, they will observe with clarity, that there is **nothing** in existence, **other than Allah**!*
>
> *This source is Allah, the Ahad. He has no partners! All other illuminations (Nur) are mere representations. The only real illumination is His Nur* (The Light of Knowledge that is the source and essence of everything). *Everything is derived from His Nur. In fact, everything is Him. The truth is, existence is Him. The engendered existence is only a metaphor, a representation. The phrase 'There is no Hu other than Hu' is the non-dual reality of the chosen ones. It leads them to unity, to Oneness!*
>
> *The last station of ascension is the realm of **soleness**. For there are no more ladders to climb after this station. Elevation can only make sense in the land of multiplicity. When multiplicity becomes obsolete, Unity becomes reality. Relativity diminishes, signs and symbols become irrelevant. At this point there are no high or low, and none who rise or fall. Progression becomes invalid, ascension becomes void. There is no more ascent beyond ascension.*
>
> *There is no multiplicity with unity. With the obliteration of multiplicity, the concept of ascension becomes nullified. He who knows this, will know; he who does not, will deny it. This*

*is an esoteric and secret knowledge only given to those who know **Allah**. When they explain this knowledge to others, only those who are arrogant towards Allah will deny.*"[13]

Based on everything we have shared so far, it is evident that the only existence is Allah! There is no other being besides Allah!

Who is making the proposal, and to whom?

The nature of this reality is such that it is like the sun, whose heat does not spare even a drop of water in the icy composition of existential reality!

Nevertheless, we cannot ignore the teachings of Muhammad (saw) in relation to the future of mankind. For, as much as Oneness is a reality, the consequences man will face in the future as a result of his own doings is also an indispensable reality.

Indeed, we are all **forms of knowledge**, in the **KNOWLEDGE** of the One denoted by the name **ALLAH**.

According to us, we are just simple creatures living in a simple universe. But, **in reality** we are just forms of knowledge in **His knowledge**!

However, since the world in our perception is a definite, absolute and multifaceted dimension, we cannot overlook the exquisite values about which we have been informed.

---

[13] This is an excerpt from Imam Ghazali's *Mishqat'ul Anwar*, an esteemed book containing esoteric knowledge. Ghazali claims he has written this book only for those of true understanding, people of deep contemplation, and not for the general public. Mishqat'ul Anwar has been translated into Turkish by Suleyman Ates and published by Mehmed Sevket Eygi of BEDIR Publications.

21

A WAY OF LIFE

The system in which we are living dictates the reality that 'there is no God who administers everything from the heavens; there is no deity-God!'

No star or planet or galaxy or constellation of stars (a star sign) can be God – to even ponder such a things is a huge misconception!

We are here, in this dimension, to fulfill our **servitude**, by executing the meanings of the names of Allah, which manifest through us.

The system in which we live comprises the Solar System, the Earth inside the Solar System, and humans who live on the Earth...

Allah has created and adorned these humans with His own attributes and designed the brain to be the place of manifestation for His qualities.

One who assumes only a bodily existence and resumes his life with this conditioning, will have to pay the consequence of this lifestyle with infinite agony and suffering.

One who trusts the locus of the knowledge of Allah, who informs him of his higher values, and who strives to discover and manifest these inner qualities, will unite with divine attributes and qualities, and attain a state of existence in which infinite beauty is experienced.

On one hand, we have an indefinite state of suffering, resulting from a lifestyle based on the mistaken assumption that man is comprised of flesh and bones (mind-body). On the other hand, we have an infinite state of serenity and pleasure resulting from manifesting the divine qualities and attributes within.

This is why **Muhammad** (saw) says:

"You have been created as **Allah's vicegerent on earth**. You have been endowed with the meanings of all of Allah's Names. Just because you are now in this material dimension of existence, do not assume that you are composed of only this physical body that will deteriorate one day. Do not 'oppress yourself' by thinking this way! Do not squander your potential! Do not waste your infinite supreme qualities for the mortal world and worldly things that you will have to leave behind one day..."

Let us look at how the following verses are warning us:

"Know that the life of this world is but amusement and diversion and adornment and boasting to one another and competition in increase of wealth and children." (Quran 57:20)

"And no friend will be in the state to call another friend, when they are shown to each other, the guilty ones will want to offer their sons as ransom (to the fire) **to be saved from the punishment of that Day** (period), **and his wife and his brother and his nearest kindred who shelter him and everything on earth so that it could save him. No! Indeed, it is the Laza** (smokeless flame)." (Quran 70:10-15)

"People are asleep, with death they will awaken!"

Indeed, the life of this world is going to seem like only a dream in the next abode. They let us die before dying so that we can awaken from this world-dream while still here! Let us see the reality and shape our lives according to these realities!

Let us not waste our energy over things that are not going to have any value in the next dimension, things that we are going to leave behind. Let us not feel remorse for squandering things that we will not be able to recompense. Confining our existence to this body and resuming a life driven by bodily desires will result in nothing but loss and disappointment... When we make the transition to the next dimension, we will say 'if only we could go back and do the things we didn't do' but this will never be possible!

In relation to this, the Quran says:

"**And that Day** (period) **Hell will be brought** (to enclose the earth)– **that Day man will remember and think, but what good to him will be the remembrance** (*dhikr*) **be** (when he no longer has a body – brain with which he can develop himself)? **He will say "I wish I had done beneficial things** (for this life)." (Quran 89:23-24)

"**Indeed we have warned you of a near punishment** (death)! **On that day, man will observe what his hands have put forth, and those who denied the knowledge of reality will say 'Oh, how I wish I were dust!'"** (Quran 78:40)

Adorn yourself with the attributes of Allah, abandon your relative self (I-ness) and become adorned with His meanings. Rid your consciousness from your illusory self so that you may attain the true SELF!

If you can truly erase your constructed self, who you have assumed into existence because of certain beliefs and conditionings, with true knowledge, such that you become free of the veil of **selfhood** (I-ness), the true Self will reveal itself.

Parallel to Muhammad's (saw) warnings, many acclaimed saints (*waliyy*) have also said:

"**Remove your self to see the Self.**"

Actually, the meaning of this expression is the same as that of the hadith "**He who knows himself, will know his *Rabb*** (the reality of the Names comprising his essence)."

Let's remember the system in which we live and how we are connected to it.

Everything we see and know in this material world is subject to the gravitational and magnetic pull of the earth. Since humans came into existence on the Earth, they too are bound by its magnetic field.

"We have created every living thing from water." (Quran 21:30)

Hence, humans too, are created from water! Now, if human beings come into existence on the Earth and are subject to Earth's gravitation, then the holographic wave body produced by the brain, commonly known as the **spirit**, must also be subject to the pull of gravity.

On the other hand, there is a quality in the human brain which, when activated, the person can become unconstrained by the magnetic field of both the Earth and the sun. As such, he can attain a **heavenly** state of existence in the dimensional depths of the infinite number of stars in space, adopting a form that is appropriate to this new dimension.

If one's anti-gravity wave producing circuit has been activated in his brain, he will assume an **illumined** (*Nur*) body, that is, a radial body, with which he is going to be able to reach salvation much more swiftly.

If, on the other hand, his brain is not able to produce antigravity waves and upload it to his spirit, due to lack of *Nur* (light of knowledge) he will neither be able to escape the magnetic field of the earth, nor hell, becoming imprisoned inside the sun forever. As, eventually the sun will engulf the five planets in its near orbit, including Mars, then shrink and become a neutron star. Hence, everything inside is going to become trapped. I have covered this topic in detail in *The Mystery of Man*, for those who may be interested.

As for the creatures (demons) living in hell, i.e. the sun... That is, the creatures that distress, humiliate and torture their captives... Just like there are people living on earth, and there are the jinn, who live on Earth or in space, every planet has its own inhabitants. Thus, the sun is also inhabited by its own unique beam-like tenants, described in the Quran as "**the demons of hell**" (*zabani[14]*).

Humans are as the strongest tenants of the Earth. We treat the weaker creatures as we like. In the same light the tenants of the sun will treat humans, the weaker creatures, however they like. This will be like torture for humans.

The spirit, or the holographic wave body, will become deformed, shrunken and burnt when consumed by the sun, due to extreme levels of radiation, but it will not cease to exist!

This is similar to our bodies being hurt and injured in our dreams but continuing to function regardless. As such, our wave bodies in the Solar-hell[15] are going to be demolished, squashed, elongated, stretched, flattened, destroyed, burnt, then restored to their original state. And this will go on indefinitely. This is confirmed by the verse:

> "So that they may taste the punishment more, every time their skins are burnt (due to their external attachments) we will replace them with new skins (externality)." (Quran 4:56)

The important point to understand here is that **the sun will be Hell in respect of its subatomic structure!**

Just like we have a biological, material, supra atomic structure as our body, and simultaneously produce its subatomic twin body in the form of wave energy, the sun also has a subatomic twin dimension comprised of radial energy. It is this dimension that we refer to as **hell**.

Due to this, we are unable to perceive hell with our current perceptive abilities, just like we are unable to see the subatomic radial spirits, jinni and angels.

Those who have made the transition from this physical body life to the spirit-wave body life are not only able to see other spirits, but also the jinni and the angels within that dimension. In fact, they will

---

[14] They have been given the name *zabani'* in the Quran.
[15] Please refer to *The Mystery of Man* for more information.

see the beings in the sun as though they are right there, next to them, for the concept of space does not apply to spirit beings. The references about the deceased watching hell from their graves pertains to this reality. Again, all of this has been covered in detail in *The Mystery of Man*.

Indeed, the heavens contained within the stars we call the Milky Way are also in respect of their wave twins comprising their subatomic dimensions.

However, just like our current plane of existence feels like a material dimension to us, based on our physical body's perceptive abilities, the next dimension is also going to feel like a physical place, even though it is a wave dimension according to our perception right now.

As for the holographic wave bodies (spirits) that make it to the countless planets in space comprising the **heavens**, they are going to have the opportunity to interact with other spirits and take part in all kinds of activities with their enhanced skills and potential. For lack of better words, they will be like the gods of the planets on which they live. For they will be Allah's vicegerents on earth, equipped and adorned with countless divine potentials, whereas the tenants of those planets lack such abilities. Thus, those who go to **heaven** will experience things that no eye has seen, no ear has heard and no tongue has spoken. Whatever we say pertaining to this topic, it will always be inadequate.

Those who go to heaven will be ageless. Relations such as parents-grandparents, sister-brother, daughter-son will be obsolete. Everyone there will be the same age. Those at the same level of power and knowledge will be together, while those who were able to acquire less knowledge and energy will reside in their own environment.

Maybe someone very close to you in this world is going to be very far from you in the next. Regardless of what you live the day before, oblivious of what you dream of the night before, when you wake up in the morning, especially after a few hours, what do they mean to you? Do they hold any validity? Yesterday is yesterday; the night before is now past. If you were in a prison cell being tortured and you fell asleep to see the most beautiful dream, what would your dream mean to you in your waking environment?

When you close your eyes to this material world and open your eyes in the next, what will this worldly life mean to you other than just a dream? Indeed, we are going to feel like we have just woken up from a deep sleep, and this worldly life and everything witnessed here is going to mean nothing, we are going to be stuck with the conditions of that environment instead!

Then our biggest concern should be, not for those things we will leave behind, but for those things that we will need in the life after death. What we plant into our spirits in the field of this world, is what we will reap in the life after death!

If, in this worldly life, we fail to recognize and use the divine qualities and potential with which we have been endowed, after tasting death, we will have lost this chance forever. There are many verses in the Quran confirming this:

> "**...when death comes to one of them, he says, 'My *Rabb*, send me back (to worldly life) so that I might do righteousness in that which I left behind (i.e. a faithful life which I did not heed or give importance to; the potential that I did not utilize and activate).'**

> "**No!** (It is impossible to go back!) **His words are invalid!** (His request is unrecognized in the system) **and behind them is a barrier** (an isthmus, a difference of dimension) **until the Day they are resurrected** (they cannot go back; reincarnation, being re-born for another worldly life is not possible!)." (Quran 23:99-100)

> "**If you could but see when they are made to stand before the fire and will say 'Oh, if only we can go back** (to life on earth) **and not deny the signs of our *Rabb*** (our intrinsic divine qualities and potential deriving from the Names that comprise our essential reality) **and be among the believers.'**

"**But that which they concealed before** (the knowledge of reality with which that had been endowed) **has now become apparent to them. And even if they were returned they would return to the things from which they had been forbidden, they are liars indeed.**

"**And they say, 'There is none but our worldly life, and we will not be resurrected.'**

"**If you could but see when they will be made to stand before their *Rabb*** (when they recognize and become aware of the potentials of the Names within their own reality). **He will say, 'Is this not the Reality?' They will say, 'Yes, it is our *Rabb*.' He will then say, 'So taste the punishment now as the consequence of denying the knowledge of reality.'**" (Quran 6:27-30)

But what is the reality of death anyway?

22

THE REALITY OF DEATH

Sadly, for many, the reality of **death** is unknown; it is thought of as an **end**. Far from it! **Death** is a transition from the material dimension to the immaterial dimension. It is a transformation.

With **death**, the person leaves his material body and continues to live with his **holographic radial-wave body**, i.e. **spirit** in the grave or beyond it. In short, death is the end of life with the material body to commence a life with the spirit body. The Quran brings clarity to the process known as death with the following verse:

> "**Every individual consciousness will taste death** (life without a biological body)." (Quran 3:185)

Death is abandoning the biological material body to live **with the spirit body** at the level of waves.

When the brain ceases to function, the electromagnetic energy, which keeps the spirit connected to the body, stops being supplied, causing the spirit to detach and continue its life independent of the body. This is the event we refer to as **death**.

Since every activity that occurs in the brain throughout one's lifetime is uploaded to the holographic wave body (as television waves are through audio and visual waves) the person will continue his life as the spirit without feeling any difference. He will live as the spirit and won't feel any difference in terms of the continuity of his life, albeit for one exception. He will not be able to use his physical body despite being completely alive and conscious! It will be as though he is in a coma or in a vegetative state, whereby he can see, hear and perceive everything that is happening around him, yet he is unable to show any response!

In his acclaimed *Marifatname*, Ibrahim Hakki Erzurumi narrates the following about death, in the words of Muhammad (saw):

> **"The deceased will know who washes and shrouds his body, who partakes in his funeral prayer, who puts him down in his grave, and who offers condolences."**

The warning '**Do not beat your chest and cry out loud near your dead, as by doing this you will be torturing them**' is again alluding to the fact that the deceased are able to hear and become grieved by all the mourning.

Perhaps the Bukhari collection of hadith comprises the most explicate narrations in clarifying the reality of death and life after death. There are many hadith affirming that the deceased, though unable to use his physical body, will be fully aware and conscious in the grave as the **spirit** and will be able to perceive all that transpires around him. Here is an example:

Narrated by Talha (r.a.):

The day of the battle of *Badr*, Rasulullah (saw) ordered us to gather the corpse of twenty of *Quraysh*'s notable men and throw their bodies down a dirty well. As such, the dirty well had gathered more dirt.

It was Rasulullah's (saw) custom to spend three nights on the field of battle once he was victorious over the enemy. So on the third day after the battle of *Badr*, Rasulullah (saw) asked for his camel. We tied his bag to the camel and Rasulullah (saw) began to walk as we followed him. The men talked amongst each other trying to guess where Rasulullah (saw) was going. Finally, he stopped by the well in which we had thrown the corpses and called out to them with their fathers' names.

"O such and such, o Aba Jahl ibn Hisam, o Utba ibn Rabia... If you had believed in and obeyed Allah and His Rasul would you have been happy now? O slayed ones! We truly found the victory promised by our *Rabb*. Did you also find the victory promised by your *Rabb* to be the truth?"

Upon this, Omar (r.a.) asked Rasulullah (saw) "O Rasulullah, why do you talk to the corpses who are dead?"

Rasulullah (saw) answered:

"By the One in whose hands the soul of Muhammad is, you do not hear my words better than they do!"[16]

As can be seen from this hadith, Rasulullah (saw) is trying to correct a big misunderstanding regarding death. No other hadith can correct the misconception that **people are dead when placed into their graves and will only be resurrected back to life on Doomsday**. Indeed, **people will be as aware and conscious as they are now when they are buried and will be able to hear everything that is told to them, just as they would if they were outside**.

The third Khalifa Osman bin Affan (r.a.) stood near a grave he would cry until his beard got soaked. Someone once said to him "You do not weep when you hear about heaven and hell but you cry in fear of the grave". He replied: "I heard Rasulullah (saw) say:

'The grave is the first station of the afterlife, if one is able to pass this station the rest of his journey will be easier, but if one cannot pass this station, the rest of his journey will be much difficult.'"

Then he added, "Rasulullah (saw) said,

'I have never encountered a scene more frightening than that of the grave.'"

---

[16] Sahih Bukhari

Standing before the grave of one of Islam's most distinguished martyrs, Sa'd bin Muaz, who Rasulullah (saw) buried with his own hands, Rasullulah (saw) said:

"**This eminent soul for whom the throne (*arsh*) trembled and the gates of the heavens opened and thousands of angels descended... Even he fret so much in his grave that his bones were almost going to crumble. If anyone were to escape from the torments of the grave and the anguish after death, this would have been possible for Sa'd first! Though, due to the elevated rank he had acquired here, he was swiftly released!**"

Let us now have a think, if the person isn't aware and conscious in his grave, could such torments be possible?

It was asked to Rasulullah (saw): "O Rasulullah, which of the believers are more intelligent and more conscious?" He answered:

"**Those who remember the reality of death most often and who prepare for the after death most prudently. Indeed, they are the most intelligent and conscious ones.**"

In yet another narration, he says: "**The most conscious and prudent one is he who subjects his soul to the divine laws and engages in deeds that will benefit him in the hereafter. The impotent one is he who follows his desires then hopes for salvation from Allah!**"

Ibn Masud, one of the followers of Rasulullah (saw) says: "I had heard Rasulullah (saw) say '**the sinners will assuredly be tormented in their graves, in fact even the animals will hear their anguish!**'"

Abu Said al Hudri narrates:

I heard Rasulullah say:

"The denier will be tormented by ninety nine dragons that will sting and bite him until the Day of Judgment. If only one of these dragons were to blow on earth, no green plant would ever live again."

Ibn Omar (r.a.) narrates:

Rasulullah (saw) said:

"When a person dies, his place, whether it be heaven or hell, will be shown to him every morning and every evening. He will be told, 'this is your place, until the Day of Judgment, when you will be resurrected, you will be here.'"

Another interesting note is the statement *"wal bat'thu ba'dal mawt"* in *Amantu*, which literally means "… and in resurrection after **death**", it does not say "resurrection after **Doomsday**"! Evidently, *ba'th*, i.e. **resurrection**, is an event that occurs after tasting death, not after Doomsday!

We live in this world without physical bodies and the spirit body that we simultaneously produce. The eminent Islamic scholar and Sufi Saint Imam Ghazali explains the name *'Al-Ba'ith'* in his *Construal of the Most Beautiful Names* as the following:

> *"Many fall into misconceptions in regards to this topic and then try to justify their beliefs, saying things like: 'death is nothingness, resurrection (ba'th) is to come back to life after becoming inexistent, just like the first time we are brought to life…' First of all, to think death is nothingness is incorrect. Secondly, to assume resurrection will be like the first time is also incorrect.*
>
> *To think of death as nothingness is wrong because the grave is either a pit of hell or a garden of paradise. Those who have been illumined to the essence of reality know and understand with insight that man has been created for eternity. Never can nothingness be attributed to it. Yes, sometimes the connection ceases with the body and they say he has died, and*

sometimes the connection is given back and they say he has come to life.

Those who think resurrection will be like the first creation have been wronged in their assumption. For, resurrection comprises an act of creation much different to that of the first time. In truth, man resurrects many times, not only twice."

When one tastes of death, the material body will dissolve and the spirit will resurrect and continue to live in the grave until Doomsday.

When Doomsday occurs, that is, the instance that the earth is engulfed in the radioactive heat of the sun...

And finally, our bodies will also be resurrected appropriate to the environment to which they will go.

Will we work with the same mind and perception mechanisms we have here in our graves?

In regards to this, Abdullah bin Omar (r.a.) narrates the following:

When Rasulullah (saw) was talking about *Munkir* and *Nakir*, the two angels who will call the person to account in his grave, Hadhrat Omar (r.a.) asked: **"Are we going to be conscious in our graves, O Rasulullah?"**

"Indeed, exactly as you are today," Rasulullah (saw) answered.

So what happens when a person, who is fully aware and conscious, yet whose body has become dysfunctional, is placed the grave?

Let us see how Anas (r.a.) has to say about this:

Rasulullah (saw) said:

"When the person is placed in his grave he will hear the footsteps of those who buried him moving further and further away. Then the two angels will come and ask him: 'What do you say about the man Muhammad?'

If the person is a believer he will say 'I bear witness that Muhammad is Allah's servant and Rasul.' Then they will ask 'Look at your place in hell, Allah has transformed it into paradise for you.' From that point on, he will see both his place in hell and the place he will go to in heaven.

If he is a denier or a hypocrite disguised as a Muslim, he will say 'I do not have a definite opinion, I only know of what others used to say.' They will say to him 'You have failed to recognize and know him!' and then they will hit him with a hammer with such intensity that the whole of creation except man and the jinni will hear his anguish!"

Let us now end this topic with a final hadith:

"The deceased one will be tormented by the lamenting of his relatives and friends."

There are many more warning of Rasulullah (saw) pertaining to this topic. Those who are interested may consult the appropriate hadith books.

The point is, **the person does not die, he merely experiences death!**

To experience death is to lose control over one's material body and to continue living with a sort of holographic wave body, termed **spirit**.

Therefore, everyone who is buried is fully conscious and aware! And they will exist in this state until Doomsday, after which they will be equipped with new bodies according to the environment and conditions of that time and place.

What happens when death is experienced?

As we said, the person continues to perceive the world around him, he hears and sees everything that is spoken and done in his immediate environment; he hears the lamenting of his relatives as though he is right next to them. At this stage, he is in a vegetative state. He perceives everything but is unable to show any response whatsoever. Then comes the time for his body to get washed.

Why do the deceased get washed?

My understanding of the wisdom pertaining to washing the corpse is related to bioelectrical energy. That is, through osmosis, the bioelectrical energy of the body becomes reinforced , so that it's life continues at the molecular level. As such, the person is able to keep a connection (even if one-way) with the world for a little while longer.

The dimension of life pertaining to the period between death and judgment day is termed **the realm of *barzakh***. This period is divided into three stages:

    a.   The life of the grave (*kabr*)

    b.   The life of the **realm of the grave**

    c.   The life of *barzakh*

A. The life of the grave

This stage of life begins when the person tastes death and is resurrected as the spirit (holographic wave) body and goes on as the person continues to perceive things as matter in the grave. The person continues to hear and see everything before and after he is buried in his grave. This is similar to going to bed but still being awake and able to perceive everything, to feel the stiffness or softness of the bed, etc. Just like this, the deceased will initially be able to see everything that transpires in his grave. And just like before we fall asleep when we seem to be in a semi-sleep state where we can still hear what is going on around us yet also begin to see dream-like things, the deceased will also continue to perceive the outside world while getting ready to make the transition into the **realm of the grave**.

This is when the two angels[17] will come to call the person to account, asking him 'Who is your *Rabb*? Who is your *Nabi*? What is your Book?'…

---

[17] *Munkir* and *Nakir*

Note that the person will never be questioned of his **sect** or **order**[18] ! **He who preaches that people will be questioned about their religious sects and Sufi orders, etc. are clearly ignorant in religious knowledge. There is no verse in the Quran, nor any recorded hadith about being questioned about one's religious sect or order!** Such establishments were formed after Rasulullah's (saw) transition to the realm of *barzakh*; these terms are not even recognized in *barzakh*!

After being held to account, the person progresses to either the **realm of the grave** or the **realm of *barzakh***. So what is the difference between the two?

B. The life of the realm of the grave

This realm is very similar to the dream world; however, the person is unaware of the fact that he is dreaming and continues to evaluate things as though he is living in the world.

The life in the realm of the grave will be perceived as real as this world is perceived when one lives here. This life can either be the **grave of heaven**, full of peaceful, serene and pleasurable dreams, or be the **grave of Hell** and comprise terrifying and agonizing nightmares.

This state of existence continues until Doomsday. This is the life of the grave of those who are confined to their graves, referenced by Rasulullah's (saw) hadith **"the grave of the deceased will either be a garden of paradise or a pit from hell."** Other than this, there is also the life of *barzakh*.

C. The realm of *barzakh*

This state of existence is **independent** of the restrictions of the grave and pertains to the saints (*waliyy*), Nabis, and those who were martyred in the name of Allah. In short, it is for those who were able to **die before dying**.

---

[18] *Mazhab* and *Tariqah*

In the realm of *barzakh*, the martyrs, saints (*waliyy*) and Nabis are able to freely roam about and, depending on their ranks, interact with each other.

Additionally, there is a hierarchy in this realm, by which the people there are administered. I have covered this topic in detail in *The Mystery of Man*, in the chapter about the '*Rijali Ghayb* (The Men of the Unseen).

The saints (*waliyy*) of *barzakh*, who were able to acquire a *fath* (self-conquest) while on earth, will be able to make contact with the people on earth. In contrast, those who were able to acquired *kashf* (self-discovery) but not *fath*, despite their freedom and unconstrained state of existence, will not have the opportunity to make such contacts.[19]

Hence, **the person will continue to live after tasting death, either in the life of the grave, or depending on his rank, in** ***barzakh***.

Such is the life awaiting us on the other side!

---

[19] More information on *'fath'* and *'kashf'* can be obtained in *A Guide To Prayer And Dhikr*.

23

PRAYER IS FOR YOU!

If all this is true…

Then please ask yourselves 'am I ready for the life awaiting me after death?'

Does your answer please you?

If it doesn't, then perhaps now is a good time to start preparing.

But what does **preparing for the afterlife** entail?

Previously we had talked about **prayer** and how it is related to the bioelectrical and biochemical make-up of the brain. In truth, most prayers serve to replenish the brain's bioelectrical energy supply, for this energy is evaluated by the brain, and uploaded to the wave-body, as knowledge and power. Due to this, when the brain stops working and becomes deactivated, i.e. when death is **tasted**, **prayer** becomes obsolete. This is why the offers proposed by *sharia (Islamic laws)* lose validity in the afterlife. For all proposals related to what is apparent have to do with the bioelectrical and biochemical structure of the brain.

The Islamic faith rests first and foremost upon the foundation of 'knowing Allah' and then preparation for the afterlife.

Allah's Rasul (saw) taught people how to live according to the Islamic faith and warned them against the losses they will incur if they don't. However, there is no creed for being accountable for which governmental regime one follows. **One's faith does not depend on the regime of the government**. If that were the case, no one on the face of the earth should be a Muslim, as there is no government observing an Islamic regime! We should be mindful of the hadith "**The *khalifat* system will last 30 years after me**" and remember that religion is for the individual, there will be no government in the life after death; there will only be the individual!

We must all try and understand, practice and teach Islam to others. For most assuredly, every person is going to have to face the consequences of his actions. All acts in the name of prayer are for the sole purpose of preparing the spirit-body for its journey after death.

Let us now briefly discuss what **prayer** actually entails and the different types of prayer:

1. Prayers to free you from confining your existence to the body alone.

2. Prayers that supply beneficial bioelectrical energy to the brain.

3. Prayers that upload the brain's existing bioelectrical energy to the holographic wave body termed the **spirit**.

4. Prayers that enable **reaching Allah or uniting with Allah**, also referred to in Sufism as **to become moralized with the morals of Allah**. In other words, to become one with the universal cosmic consciousness.

As can be seen from this brief categorization, all activity pertaining to prayer is related to the **brain**.

While the brain takes the bioelectrical energy it needs and uploads it to the spirit it also emits it, in the form of meanings, to its environment in the world.

If the necessary circuitry has been activated in one's brain during birth, then he will be able to upload a sort of anti-gravitational, anti-magnetic energy, which will enable him to soar to the countless stars within the galaxy, freeing him from the magnetic field of the Earth and the sun during Doomsday.

Otherwise, he will be doomed to entrapment within the sun for eternity.

"You will never see a deviation in Sunnatullah (the mechanics of Allah's system)." (Quran 35:43)

This verse is a clear proof that the system of Allah is applicable to the whole of humanity. It has been set up and working for billions of years! In this case, the individual has two options: either to order his life according to the system; live his worldly life by making use of certain practices to enable benefits in his future. Or, to not think about the future or the system at all, to live a life driven by bodily activities.

Those who fail to recognize the reality of **religion**, or **the system that enables preparation for life after death**, misconceive religion as a system through which the masses are managed and kept under control. This, of course, goes as far as involving governmental regimes into the topic! Whereas, I repeat, religious prayers and practices are solely related to the requirements of the afterlife, **not** the regimes of worldly life.

As a matter of fact, Muhammad (saw) spent his entire life in pursuit of communicating the following messages:

    a. Allah is not a deity-God; to worship Allah (by deifying, offering, etc.) is absolutely impossible because it does not exist!

    b. All activities carried out by the individual are the compulsory requirements of his servitude and not forms of worshipping a deity-God.

    c. Prayer should not be directed to a heavenly (external) God in hopes of ingratiating one's self with Him, but to prepare for a favorable future of eternity.

d. The individual should die before dying in order to be cleansed from his constructed illusory self and to know his essence, origin, creator, Allah.

Otherwise, it is inevitable for the person to die veiled from reality, a state from which he will never have the chance to escape.

Indeed, let us know and understand with certainty that the teachings disclosed by **Muhammad** (saw) in the name of **religion**, are way beyond the stories and superstitious tales passed on from generation to generation among the general public.

Future generations will have a much clearer understanding of **ALLAH** and what it signifies.

In fact you will realize the validity of these truths once you take the time to conduct some personal research into related scientific resources and reflect on your findings.

24

WHAT IS *DHIKR?*

Religion is not for attaining worldly sovereignty. In Jesus' words, it is **to attain "the kingdom of heaven."** And this is only possible by reaching **the essential reality of one's self.**

How can one attain knowledge of the **self?**

Via the brain, of course!

Our success will be determined by the extent to which we use our brain's capacity. The wider the scope of our reflective capacity, the more objectively we can view things and the stronger our spirits will get, allowing us to know the reality of Allah.

But how will such progress take place in the brain?

As I have thoroughly explained in my book *A Guide To Prayer And Dhikr*, through the practice known as *dhikr!*

Indeed, *dhikr* is the key to all of the above.

Primarily, *dhikr* is known to be a repetition of certain prayers and names of **Allah**. Its second meaning entails **remembrance and to reflect on.** Furthermore, it means to elaborate and dwell on a meaning such that it yields deep, comprehensive contemplation.

Here are some verses from the Quran in regards to the importance of *dhikr*:

"O believers! Let not your worldly goods or your children make you oblivious of the remembrance of Allah (the remembrance of your essential self, and the necessary practices that accompany this). And whoever does this – it is they who are the losers!" (Quran 63:9)

"They (the objects/idols of their worship) will say, '*Subhan*[20] you are! It is not possible for us to take besides You any allies. But when You provided comforts for them and their fathers, they forgot the knowledge of reality and indulged in bodily pleasures eventually leading to their ruin.'" (Quran 25:18)

"And whoever is blinded (with external things) from remembering that his essential composition is composed of the names of Allah, and thus from living the requirements of this, (*Rahman*) We appoint for him a devil (a delusion; the idea that he is only the physical body and that life should be lived in pursuit of bodily pleasures) and this (belief) will become his (new) identity! And indeed, these will avert them from the way [of guidance; the path to reality] while they think that they are [rightly] guided!" (Quran 43:36-37)

"Satan (corporeality; the idea of being just the physical body) has overcome them and made them forget the remembrance of Allah (their own reality of which they have been reminded, and that they will abandon their bodies and live for eternity as 'consciousness' comprised of Allah's names!) Those are the acquaintances of Satan (the advocates of corporeality, those who only think of themselves as the physical body). Beware, for most assuredly, the party of Satan will be the very losers!" (Quran 58:19)

The absence of remembrance in the form of *dhikr* is probably the biggest lack in our lives. Those whose brains are deprived of the power of *dhikr* are easily susceptible to the manipulations of the jinni.

---

[20] The One who creates a new manifestation every instance and is absolutely free from becoming confined or limited by them.

Being under the influence of Satan denotes a much bigger reality than one may assume. The Quran clearly states that **the majority of the human race is under the direct manipulation of the jinni:**

> "**The day when Allah resurrects them all, He will say to them: 'O community of jinn, you have truly possessed** (misled from reality) **most of mankind.**'" (Quran 6:128)

The only and most powerful weapon man has against the jinni, who appear most often in the guise of **aliens** or **extraterrestrial beings**, is *dhikr*.

The most observable feature of those who are under the influence of the jinni is the absurdity of their speech, which lacks logical uniformity and is contradictory.

The Quran advises reciting the following verses as a *dhikr* or as prayer to be protected from them:

> "*Rabbi inni massaniyash shaytanu bi nusbin we adhab; Rabbi audhu bika min hamazatish shayatini wa audhu bika Rabbi an yahdurun wa hifzan min kulli shaytanin marid*" (Quran 38:41, 23:97-98, 37:7)

> "**He called to his *Rabb*** (the reality of the Names comprising his essence), **'Indeed, Satan** (the feeling of being this body) **has given me hardship and torment.**'"

> "**And say, 'My *Rabb*! I seek refuge in You** (the protective names within my essence) **from the incitements of the devils** (that call to corporeality). **And I seek refuge in You** (the protective names within my essence) **my *Rabb*, lest they be present with me.**'"

> "**We protected the nearest heaven** (earth's atmosphere) **from every rebellious satan.**"

Cigarettes are the most prominent source of smoke nutrition for the **jinni**. Due to this they never leave the presence of smokers.

Again, *dhikr* **and prayer** is the only way one can protect the self from their influences.

Prayer and *dhikr* enable the brain to produce a protective energy, which can shield the brain from the impulses sent by the jinni, either by weakening these incoming impulses or by preventing them altogether.

In fact, the protective energy omitted by the brain during *dhikr* **forms a field of protection around the person.**

Indeed, our preeminent purpose in life should be to develop and enhance our brain via *dhikr* and thereby to know our selves and our environment. For **our brain possesses potential that is beyond our imagination.** If only we could harness its power!

Only then may we gain insight into the reality of man, his make-up, his mechanism, his inherent qualities and how to optimize them through *dhikr* and prayer.

25

THE VEIL OF CONDITIONING

The biggest obstacle preventing us from accomplishing our purposes and **veiling** the reality is **conditionings**. Our conditionings can make us as absurd as a man looking for his glasses when all the time they are sitting on his head. Indeed, **until man is cleansed from his conditionings, and the value judgments and emotions that result from them,** he can never truly know the One denoted by the name Allah. As such, he can never attain the reality of his self, nor know **Allah as disclosed by Muhammad** (saw).

He will utter the word **Allah** throughout his whole life, yet this will be the name given to the God created in his mind, the God he imagined based on his conditionings! Someone who fails to comprehend the Allah revealed by Muhammad (saw), can say **Allah to the God he imagines and creates** in his mind – as a result of a lifestyle driven by conditionings and instincts – all he likes, this will be of no benefit to him at all. For **Duality is most certainly the worst form of self-oppression!**

One who fails to recognize and comprehend Allah, as disclosed by Muhammad (saw), has no chance at knowing the origin of his consciousness, to leap into the dimension of cosmic consciousness, or to evaluate the universe in light of its actual reality! For the imaginary God in his head will forever keep him cocooned and prevent him from perceiving the reality for what it really is.

The only way one can escape the cocoon of his conditionings is by receiving and contemplating upon the knowledge of reality and complying with its requirements.

Sadly, however, people generally do not know how to use their inherent contemplative skills and are instead raised as rote learners. As such, they do not want or like to be involved in anything that requires deeper thinking. Due to this, they behave according to their environment, conforming to the ways of hearsay and imitating the things others do. As a result, everybody **worships his own deity!** From a very young age we become conditioned to believe that whatever the adults around us do must be the right thing, and hence we do the same; we adopt their values as our own. These values then drag us into assuming things that are totally contradictory to reality, trapping us inside a cocoon weaved from delusion and making us think: 'Why should I spend my whole life worshipping God when I can just do something nice later and win His favor to escape?'

All such thoughts are inappropriate assumptions based on false information obtained via baseless conditionings! The Quran refers to such people as:

"**They follow only assumption and what** [their] **souls desire** (though) **the knowledge of Reality has indeed come to them from their** *Rabb* (the reality of the Names comprising their essence)." (Quran 53:23)

"**And they have no knowledge thereof. They follow only assumptions, and indeed, never can assumption reflect the truth**." (Quran 53:28)

"**And your assumption about your** *Rabb* **has brought you to perdition, and you have become among the losers**." (Quran 41:23)

Indeed, nothing can compensate for the loss caused by incorrect conditionings!

We confine ourselves **to the flesh-bone body** and **assume the existence of a God up in the heavens** and then we attempt to **worship him with this bodily personality!** We get upset with this

God, we judge and criticize Him, and more often than not, we blame Him for doing inappropriate things... **Never do we realize that a God like this simply cannot exist!** Never do we hear **Muhammad's** (saw) message that a God like that *does not* exist. Consequently we continue our lives making irreversible mistakes...

What if we were to consider **man's place on earth**, if we were to think about the life and place of a single human being on earth... If there were a God as big as the Earth, what will be the place of this single human being next to God? Now think about the sun, one million three hundred and thirteen thousand times bigger than the earth... What is the place of the Earth next to the sun?

What is the size of a human next to the sun? Perhaps like a chromosome in a cell compared to the whole human body. And what is the place of the sun within the galaxy that comprises 400 billion stars like the sun? If the galaxy that comprises 400 billion sun-like stars were 'God', what would be the place of the sun next to this magnificence?

Now let us imagine **the sun, worshipping this galaxy-god,** by deifying and exalting it, or, denying, resenting and getting angry at it. **What will be its effect, if any? And what will be the place of a single human being in comparison to this magnificent galaxy-god?** Let us think about this on a serious note... **For if we can see the absurdity in this picture, we can understand that prayer is not an offering-like practice, made to an external God in order to get into his good books!**

The wise and the enlightened ones of the past say:

Allah does not need any of your prayers! It is you who needs them, if you want to secure your future.

Indeed, it is not Allah who needs your prayers but you! Prayer is for you!

If we fail to give sufficient importance to prayer, we would have oppressed our selves by not enriching it with the countless qualities and powers it deserves.

Knowing and deciphering your essential self, discovering your infinite intrinsic potential and allowing yourself to live in a paradisiacal state of eternal life depends on these activities you carry out.

You must engage in these practices for your self, for your own benefit...

On the contrary, **the only one in loss will be you, for there is no God out there with whom you can ingratiate yourself!**

Beware:

If by saying 'there is no God out there' you abandon all your practices and prayers you will accrue an enormous loss. For, such practices are imperative for your future, and should never be neglected. The only misunderstanding that needs correcting is, none of these prayers and practices should be done for an external God with the intention of earning his favor, but for your very self and your future!

26

ACTIONS SPEAK LOUDER THAN WORDS!

Neither **Allah**, nor Muhammad (saw) need your faith or prayers!

Imagine a ship, sailing the ocean, full of travelers… Suddenly, the ship hits an iceberg and starts sinking. The captain makes an announcement notifying everybody that the ship is sinking and asks them to wear their life jackets or to obtain life rings. While most people heed this announcement and rush to ensure their safety, one man says: '**I believe in the captain**. I love the captain!' yet does nothing to obtain a life jacket or ring. When the ship sinks, like everybody else, he finds himself in the water, but unlike the rest, he begins to struggle and drown, yelling out to the ocean: 'Don't drown me ocean! I believe in the captain! I love the captain!'

If the ocean could talk back, it would probably say, 'If you had really believed the captain, you would have heeded his message and worn your life jacket! It is not the act of **believing** the captain, but following his instructions that would have been of benefit for you here. Merely **believing** the captain is only good for you while you're on that ship. Out here, you live the consequences of your own actions, or lack thereof! Whether you believed him or not means nothing at this point!'

Similarly, many people spend their lives saying '**I believe in Allah, I believe in Rasulullah**' but do nothing in heed of their message! In fact, they don't even feel the need to research it!

Simply saying '**I believe**' isn't what is asked of us. **Neither Allah nor Muhammad (saw) needs anyone to believe in them!**

It is required to acquire certain powers by engaging in the practices advised by Muhammad (saw) so that we may be delivered from the tribulations and torments awaiting us in the life after.

Indeed, if we *believe* **Rasulullah** (saw), and hence *follow* his instructions in realizing our intrinsic potentials, we may be saved from the state (environment) known as **Hell**.

But no matter how much we claim to believe, if we fail to walk on the path shown by Allah's Rasul, suffering from hell fire will be inescapable, as we would not have acquired what is necessary to accomplish the transition.

"[In the life to come] **all shall have their degrees in accordance with their deeds, so that He will fully compensate them for their achievements, and they will not be wronged**." (Quran 46:19)

"**This is the result of what your hands have put forth. Verily, Allah is not ever unjust to [His] servants.**" (Quran 22:10)

This being the case, do not wrong your selves by wasting your brain capital, energy, and life on things that will be rendered meaningless with death!

The verse "**Allah does not like the squanderers**" is not in reference to those who waste a little worldly capital here and there! It refers to those who waste their *souls*! It warns against wasting one's soul, or **self**, and all its intrinsic divine qualities and potential of **vicegerency**.

Many Rasuls and Nabis, are quoted throughout the Quran as saying "**I have wronged my soul, I have wronged myself**" denoting this very reality. That is, they express their concerns of doing wrong by their **selves** by not duly and adequately using their intrinsic quality of **vicegerency**.

And would it be such a loss if we were to **waste** some worldly possessions that we are bound to leave behind anyway?

If, on the other hand, we squander away something that we will need for eternity and never again have the opportunity to retrieve it, we will have done such an injustice by our **selves** that it is impossible for me to express here the remorse it will result in.

Doing wrong by your soul, which will be your source of divine life and (godly) powers in the next dimension of existence, will only result in eternal disappointment and pain.

The realities of the afterlife are completely different to the realities of this world. Let me provide an example regarding the concept of time:

The sun takes 255 million years to rotate around the center of the galaxy. Do we have any idea what this means? The Quran says one day in the afterlife will be like one thousand earth years.

> **"In the sight of your *Rabb*, one day is like one thousand (earthly) years."** (Quran 22:47)

> **"They will murmur among themselves, 'You remained (in the world) only ten [hours].'"** (Quran 20:103)

Perhaps our life in the grave is going to last millions and millions of years...

Muhammad (saw) says:

> **"It will take 3000 years for a person to cross the bridge of *Sirat*."**

That is, 3000 years each day of which is like a thousand earth years!

Crossing the *Sirat* symbolizes escaping from the magnetic pull of the sun after Doomsday and reaching the heavens in space. This will take 3000 galactic years! At this point, **Earth time** would have been rendered completely obsolete!

How much longer to Doomsday?

How many millions or billions of years more will the deceased ones have to wait in their graves?

How many billions of years will it take for the Earth to melt from the heat of the sun and become flat like a tray?

How many hundreds of millions of years will it take for people to escape this magnetic battle? And finally, how many billions and billions of years will the **eternal** afterlife comprise?

Imagine going through all of this on your own!

Imagine being prisoned in your grave and consciously watching your body being eaten by all the insects and animals under the ground for perhaps billions of years... Imagine the pain emerging from the absence of everything you possessed and were accustomed to in this world... And imagine this pain to last until Doomsday, while all the time watching the turmoil further awaiting you!

All this pertains only to the life in the grave; I'm not even going to attempt to expound the rest! Those who wish, may obtain detailed information about the stages of the afterlife from various hadith books.

Thus, man constructs his own future with his actions and deeds in this world.

We can either take this reality into serious consideration and consciously evaluate our worldly life in this light, directing our system of thoughts and lives accordingly, or ignore it all and extinguish our lives with worldly pleasures and pain.

All this depends on how much we know and understand **Allah**, as disclosed by **Muhammad** (saw).

If we genuinely want to prepare ourselves for the afterlife, we must first begin with the concept of **Allah** and truly understand it.

Labeling the Gods in our imagination **Allah** is generally the primary cause of all defective behavior.

"Have you seen the one who takes as his god his own desire (corporeality, bodily stimulations – delusion)?" (Quran 25:43)

When belief in God *based on imitation* comprises the foundation of our religious understanding it can often lead to denial or rebellion, resulting in the extreme case of total annihilation.

Whereas if only we truly understood the reality that **Allah is Ahad**, that there is no God in the heavens, and that **we will all face the consequences of our own doings**, our entire lives would completely and absolutely change!

27

UNITY OF EXISTENCE VS UNITY OF WITNESS

The controversial topics of *Unity of Existence* and *Unity in Witness* have always caused much debate amongst Islamic scholars. Nevertheless, all Islamic scholars and saints (*waliyy*) unanimously and doubtlessly believe in the **oneness** of Allah.

Ubaydullah Akhrar from the *Naqshibandi* order states "*the purpose of Sufism is the topic of Existence*" implying the sole purpose of Sufi teachings is to aid the correct comprehension of the Oneness of Allah.

The **assumption** that '**there are two ways of approaching Oneness**' has unfortunately resulted in a division among the inexpert, leading the saints (*waliyy*) to expound the matter, each according to his own station and state.

The knowledge of Allah's *Ahadiyyah* was passed on from Muhammad (saw) to Hadhrat Ali and Hadhrat Abu Bakr, then successively passed on to all the saints (*waliyy*), and finally systemized into the understanding of Oneness as **Unity of Existence** by Imam Ghazali and Muhyiddin Ibn Arabi.

Nevertheless, misunderstandings, over time, have led to incorrect interpretations of *Ahadiyyah*, resulting in the erroneous creed: '**The corporeal existence is Allah; Allah is the sum total of everything in existence.**'

One thousand years later, Ahmad Faruq Sarhandi revised this notion and relieving the **Unity of Existence** from the awry materialistic approach of **Allah is the physical existence**, he established the view: '**Allah is the *only* existence, all else are His shadows**' reinforcing the idea that nothing in the corporeal world has an independent separate existence.

To put it simply...

Based on the Quran and countless hadith, the notion of **Unity of Existence** affirms that everything in existence is in its essence no other than the existence of the **One Reality**. In other words, all of existence is essentially **one**, it only appears to be **many** because the **One** manifests Itself and Its infinite structural qualities in wondrously different ways at every instance.

In the whole of existence, there is only one source of knowledge, will and power. The existence of the cosmos is not separate or independent of Allah!

The cause of dualistic view is the veil with which intelligent beings are created, that is, humans are veiled from their essential reality so that they may actualize their purpose of creation. If no such veil existed in their intellects, every intelligent being would have been conscious of his essential values, and the perception of multiplicity, and many formations pertaining to it, would have faded.

When Ahmad Faruq Sarhandi (also known as Imam Rabbani) revised the notion of **Unity of Existence** in the year 1000 *Hijri,* a new approach was conceived:

"Existence is One... However, the observable, perceivable existence is only a shadow."

What Sarhandi means by **shadow** is that the perceivable world is like a **shadow** or like an **imagining** *in relation to the Absolute Essence* (*dhat*).

The **Absolute Essence** (*dhat*) is necessarily beyond and independent of the *perceivable existence.*

As we had covered in the section about chapter *al-Ikhlas,* the One denoted by the name **Allah is *Ahad*** in respect of His Absolute Essence, thus it is impossible to perceive Him.

This is why **Muhammad** (saw) said "**do not contemplate upon the Absolute Essence (*dhat*) of Allah!**"

This warning should not be misconstrued. He is not saying, it can be contemplated but you shouldn't. In fact, he's saying **such a contemplation is not possible!**

He is cautioning us against deviating off course through implausible contemplation. He is advising us not to waste our time by attempting unachievable things.

Let us explain why with an example:

Imagine you had many aliases through which your different skills were represented. Who do all these skills and attribute belong to? You. But who are you? You are a living, conscious and intelligent being with the will and capacity to manifest your qualities to bring them out from the state of potential to the state of tangible perceivable actions. So, if I was to ask who all these qualities belong to, you will say **me**, but who is this person **me**?

At this point, you are bound to go back! Just like when you stretch a piece of elastic you can only stretch it so far before you have to shrink it back again – at some point you must go back to the *qualities* of **me**. For whenever you attempt to explain the actual being denoted by **me** you must necessarily do so via your qualities and attributes. This is what Sufism refers to as **the return from the state of Absolute Essence to the state of the Attributes**.

Thus, it is impossible to contemplate and comprehend the Absolute Essence of Allah!

As such, **Allah the *Ahad***, testifies Himself to the fact that there is no other than He.

"*Shahid Allahu anna Hu, la ilaha illa huwa wal malaikatu wa ulul'ilm...*" (Quran 3:18)

Which means:

"Allah witnesses that He is HU, there is no deity, there is only HU... and [so do] the forces (potentials) **of His names**

(angels) **and those of knowledge** (those who manifest knowledge)…"

There is a crucial point of which we must be mindful:

To think, 'let me study about the existence, universe, space, etc. first, *then* I'll get to know the One denoted by Allah' is profoundly wrong!

In the past they used to refer to this retrospective approach as going **from the artwork to the artist**. This path is far too long, tortuous, dangerous and much too labyrinth-like! Once you embark on this journey, it is hardly possible to complete it.

There is no end to Allah's words; there is no end to the meanings denoted by Allah's names!

Hence, there is no end to the act of observing these meanings either!

This naturally brings us to the conclusion that, **there is no end to existence!**

The **end** that is proposed to existence is only **relative**, in respect to the Absolute Essence.

Manifest or **unmanifest** knowledge are **not sufficient to allow the recognition and application of this reality**.

External knowledge comprises all the sciences and areas of knowledge that depend on the five senses, including the science of symbology.

Internal knowledge incorporates everything that is beyond the five senses, that is, introspective knowledge based on intrinsic observation and discovery. Neither is sufficient to enable one to duly know Allah and live the reality.

Living and experiencing the **reality** is only possible through *ilm-i ladun* (knowledge disclosed directly from the presence of **Allah**). For the realization of Divine Attributes is only possible through *ilm-i ladun*.

In Sufi terms, the primary purpose is to know one's self at the level of the Names, Attributes and Essence, and this can only be done when the point of destination is comprehended and its requirements are fulfilled.

Thus, the first place to start is **knowing and understanding the One denoted by the name Allah!**

When the journey begins from Allah, and goes to Allah, with Allah, it becomes increasingly short!

To conclude, the point is not to reach Allah via the creation, but to know the One denoted as Allah and observe the creation *with His view*. Otherwise, we will spend our lives wondering about in creation, **veiled** and unable to transgress the **curtains** that conceal the reality!

May **Allah** enable us to constantly engage in contemplation, to become free from assumptions, to attain the reality, and to realize our intrinsic divine realities and qualities.

AHMED HULUSI

14 November 1989
Antalya

ABOUT THE AUTHOR

Ahmed Hulusi (Born January 21, 1945, Istanbul, Turkey) contemporary Islamic philosopher. From 1965 to this day he has written close to 30 books. His books are written based on Sufi wisdom and explain Islam through scientific principles. His established belief that the knowledge of Allah can only be properly shared without any expectation of return has led him to offer all of his works which include books, articles, and videos free of charge via his web-site. In 1970 he started examining the art of spirit evocation and linked these subjects parallel references in the Quran (smokeless flames and flames instilling pores). He found that these references were in fact pointing to luminous energy which led him to write *Spirit, Man, Jinn* while working as a journalist for the Aksam newspaper in Turkey. Published in 1985, his work called *'Mysteries of Man (Insan ve Sirlari)'* was Hulusi's first foray into decoding the messages of the Quran filled with metaphors and examples through a scientific backdrop. In 1991 he published *A Guide To Prayer And Dhikr (Dua and Zikir)'* where he explains how the repetition of certain prayers and words can lead to the realization of the divine attributes inherent within our essence through increased brain capacity. In 2009 he completed his final work, *'The Key to the Quran through reflections of the Knowledge of Allah'* which encompasses the understanding of leading Sufi scholars such as Abdulkarim al Jili, Abdul-Qadir Gilani, Muhyiddin Ibn al-Arabi, Imam Rabbani, Ahmed ar-Rifai, Imam Ghazali, and Razi, and which approached the messages of the Quran through the secret Key of the letter 'B'.